How to Play

POPULAR PIANO

in

10 EASY

LESSONS

by Norman Monath

A FIRESIDE BOOK
Published by Simon & Schuster
New York London Toronto Sydney Tokyo Singapore

Rockefeller Center
1230 Avenue of the Americas
New York, New York 10020
FIRESIDE and colophon are registered trademarks of Simon & Schuster, Inc.
Designed by Daniel Chiel
Music Typography by Irwin Rabinowitz
Photographs by Simon Metz
Chord Diagrams by Foliographics, Inc.
Manufactured in the United States of America
Printed and bound by Semline, Inc.

23 25 27 29 30 28 26 24

Library of Congress Cataloging in Publication Data

Monath, Norman.
How to play popular piano in 10 easy lessons.

"A fireside book."
1. Piano—Instruction and study. 2. Music, Popular
(Songs, etc.)—Instruction and study. 3. Harmony,
Keyboard. 4. Improvisation (Music) I. Title.
II. Title: Popular piano.
MT239.M68   1984   786.3'041   84-10314
ISBN: 0-671-53067-4

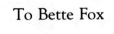
To Bette Fox

ACKNOWLEDGMENTS

I want to thank Simon Metz for his patience and professionalism in taking all the photographs used in this book. My thanks, also, to Michael Shimkin for allowing us to use his piano for that purpose.

Above all, I am grateful to Barbara Gess who, during the course of her invaluable editorial supervision, always managed to strike the right note!

CONTENTS

FOREWORD by Hal David   11
AUTHOR'S PREFACE   15

INTRODUCTION
The Principle Behind This Method   17

LESSON 1
The Piano Keyboard   23

LESSON 2
Playing Melodies   31

LESSON 3
First Chords and Songs   37

LESSON 4
Reading Black Keys From Music   49

LESSON 5
The Scales and Chords We Build On   55

LESSON 6
The Meaning of Tonality   67

LESSON 7
Altering Major Triads   71

LESSON 8
Four-Note Chords   81

LESSON 9
Jazz Piano Styles   105

LESSON 10
Playing by Ear and Improvising   123

APPENDIX
Checklist of Chord Symbols   131
Music Notation   135

FOREWORD

Promises, promises: that seems to be the name of the game these days when it comes to creating titles for self-help books. Look at the best-seller lists and you will find books that purport to show you how to make a fortune on a shoestring (in your spare time, of course) or how to lose weight while eating all of your favorite foods.

It is therefore refreshing to come across a book every so often that really fulfills the promise of its title. This is just such a book and I heartily recommend it. Take the ten lessons prescribed by the author and you will not only find them easy to understand, but fun to do as well as rewarding to follow.

Since I'm the head of an organization that derives a great deal of income from broadcasts of its music you might expect me to say: "Don't play the piano, play the radio!" However, I know that the future musical health of this country depends upon developing performers as well as listeners. This book can go a long way in turning hitherto passive appreciators into happily involved practitioners of that king of instruments—the piano—and I am happy to give it my blessing.

Hal David, President
The American Society of Composers,
Authors and Publishers

How to Play

POPULAR
PIANO

in

10 EASY
LESSONS

AUTHOR'S PREFACE

Some years ago Simon & Schuster published songbooks by such eminent songwriters as George and Ira Gershwin, Jerome Kern, Rodgers and Hart, Cole Porter, Rodgers and Hammerstein, and Bacharach and David. Since I was the music editor for those publications, I was able to keep a piano in my office in order to check proofs of the music arrangements for our special editions.

Having a piano in my office gave me the opportunity to play for my own pleasure from time to time as well as for the business of music-editing. Quite often my colleagues would pop their heads into my office and tell me how much they enjoyed hearing the great songs I was playing. "I'd give anything," they used to say, "if only I could play some of those songs." To this I always responded, "You don't have to give *anything*—just one or two lunch hours with me and I'll show you all you need to know to play your favorite songs."

At first my colleagues just couldn't believe my promise was a serious one; they couldn't believe they had the necessary talent and dexterity they thought was a prerequisite to playing piano. However, as they began, one by one, to take me up on my offer, they came to realize the truth of what I had always maintained: to play the melodies and chords* of popular songs, or hymns, or Christmas carols or folk songs requires absolutely *no* talent and only the amount of dexterity you'd need to be able to dial a telephone number.

*For a definition of the word "chord" see the first paragraph of Lesson Three.

As a result of the informal lessons I gave to my friends at Simon & Schuster, I decided to put together a mail-order course of my method. The course was to consist of some explanatory text together with a recording of me at the piano demonstrating the various ways one might put chords and melodies together to produce simple yet satisfying musical effects.

Unfortunately, I was not able to acquire the rights either to reprint parts of the sheet music or to record parts of many of the songs I wanted to use. That is, I could not acquire those rights for fees that would have been reasonable enough for me to afford, unless I priced the course at $1,000.00 retail! Also, I became involved in the formation of my own book publishing company and had to shelve many of my embryonic projects.

Thus, for some twenty-odd years I have been teaching friends how to play piano, and for the same twenty-odd years they have been imploring me to put the finishing touches on my method so that it could be made available to the general public. When my publisher recently came up with the suggestion that I write a book on the subject, I decided to dust off the mail-order package that had been sitting on the shelf and adapt it to book form. You are now reading the result, and I hope it will bring you the happiness and satisfaction that this simple method has brought to so many of my friends and colleagues.

Playing the piano can be a fun game as well as a serious profession. Traditionally, however, most people are taught to play as if they were training to become concert pianists. That approach involves all the tiresome groundwork of trills and drills that frightens off so many would-be players. I maintain that if you want to play piano just for the fun of it, it should also be fun to learn. That is the goal of this book, and what's more, if you ever do decide to pursue a professional career, what you learn here won't stop you.

The Principle Behind This Method

Imagine trying to learn how to use a typewriter if you were illiterate. No matter how bright a person you were, the only way you could learn to type a word or a simple sentence would be by rote. You would have to be shown how to type each word, and your ability to type any particular word would not be of use in learning how to type any other. Unless you learned the alphabet and how it works in spelling, you would have to look at a diagram in order to type a word as simple as CAT. Of course, with arduous practice, and memorization, an illiterate person could even learn how to type a play by Shakespeare.

You see what I'm driving at?

Traditionally, piano playing is taught by rote. The musical alphabet is ignored and the pupil never learns to "spell" chords. Of course with arduous practice, and memorization, a musical illiterate can learn to play a sonata by Beethoven or a Gershwin song; but don't ask that person to play "Jingle Bells" at Christmas—not unless you have a complicated diagram (the printed music) that he or she has learned to follow by rote.

17

Why is piano playing taught that way when we wouldn't think of teaching typing that way?

First of all, we simply have to learn our ABC's in order to communicate. As a matter of fact, it's the law of the land that we do so. In the case of music, however, it is optional as to whether we learn its "language." In fact, a four-year-old child can begin to play pieces by Mozart and Beethoven almost immediately by staying at the piano and learning how to be a good copycat. I use the word "copycat" advisedly because that expresses the essence of what it is to learn by rote.

Secondly, as far as the difference between "playing" a typewriter and a piano is concerned, we generally type our own particular sets of words or sentences rather than copy what someone else has written. In music, however, most of us try to play what someone else has composed, and so the quick, copycat approach is used. Instead of learning how Beethoven or Gershwin "spelled" their music we simply repeat what they have written without bothering to understand the underlying ABC's.

At first the rote method seems to work well, particularly with simple pieces, and for those who have a lot of patience. As we start learning more difficult pieces, however, hours and hours of tedious practice are required. Now that's fine for those who want to become concert pianists. They have to learn each and every note exactly as written by the great masters, but for those of us who simply want to play familiar melodies for fun, it's a needlessly difficult procedure to follow.

You don't have to play a song by Richard Rodgers, or Irving Berlin, or the Beatles exactly as they wrote it as you would if you wanted to play a piece by Chopin. As a matter of fact, almost all popular composers never wrote their own piano arrangements. They simply wrote out the melody and named the particular chords they had in mind for the harmony. I'll illustrate that now since it involves the basic idea behind this method.

If a simple song such as "Jingle Bells" were to be published in typical sheet-music fashion, the way the biggest hits of the past and present are printed, it might look something like this:

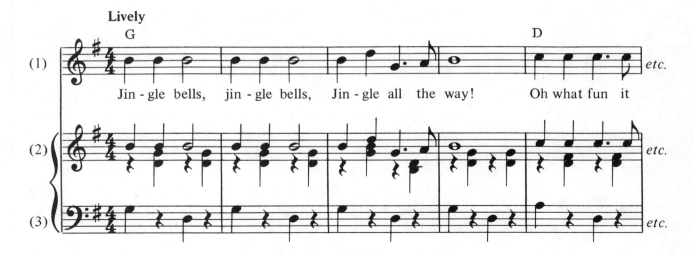

It might also look like this:

There are endless ways "Jingle Bells" can be arranged, one just as valid as another, depending upon your personal taste. Now, for a song as simple as "Jingle Bells," the simple arrangements above can look quite complicated; *frightening* as a matter of fact if you can't read notes. Even if you can read notes, but were taught the traditional, rote way, it would take hours and hours of tedious practice for you to be able to play any of those arrangements. That's because you would have to know a lot of things before you could play those notes as written. For example, you would have to know the difference between half notes and quarter notes, between rests and tied notes, between treble clef and bass clef; above all, you would have to know how to coordinate the movements of your left hand with your right.

Fortunately, you can spare yourself the necessity of having to decipher most of the hieroglyphics of music that will confront you when you look at a song. Let me illustrate what I mean by going back to "Jingle Bells." Note that each of the arrangements above involves three lines of music (I numbered them (1), (2), (3) on the left-hand side.) The two lower lines represent the piano part, line 2 the notes for the right hand and line 3 the notes for the left.

If you were playing by rote, you would have to concern yourself with lines 2 and 3. Fortunately, you won't have to bother with those lines at all. All you will look at is the top line:

The above line is called the vocal line since it is used by singers who need to see only the melody and the words. That melody is what you will be playing with your right hand, and the notes are simple to learn even if you don't already know how. As I mentioned before, you won't have to know the difference between the dark notes and light notes or what kind of stems they have. Those things have to do with the duration of each of the notes of the melody, which you already know. You will simply play those notes at the same speed or tempo as you would sing them. Instead of singing with your voice, you will be singing with your fingers. That relieves you of all the counting and tedious mathematics involved in figuring out the exact duration of each note. This way you retain the option of playing at whatever speed is comfortable and you can also play those notes with whichever fingers you choose to use—only forefinger and thumb if you don't mind resembling Chico Marx! (Actually, he was a fine pianist.)

Besides indicating the notes of the melody for your right hand, the vocal line also indicates what you should play with your left hand in order to produce the proper harmony. Refer back to the vocal line of "Jingle Bells" and you'll see a capital G above the word "Jingle" and a capital D above the word "Oh." Those letters are actually indications for guitarists so they know which chords to strum when they are accompanying the melody. The capital G stands for a G chord, D for a D chord, etc. Those chord letters can also be used by you as a guide in deciding what to play with your left hand.

I say "as a guide" because once you learn the various chords, you may decide to play chords of your own choosing rather than follow the printed designations. You will understand why this is possible before you finish reading this book. For now, suffice it to say that popular music is very flexible and allows performers many options with respect to melody, harmony and rhythm. When you sing, whistle or hum a song, you don't always stick to the exact notes, particularly if you're trying to add a little of your own expressiveness to the music. Likewise, you don't have to play the exact notes that are indicated if you feel like doing something else at that moment. It is only when you are playing by rote that you have to be rigid, that you are handcuffed to the piano part as spelled out in the two lines (*staves*, if you want to be technical) which are under the vocal line.

Once again, look at the piano part of the first example of "Jingle Bells." That merely represents one possible way of arranging the notes of G and D chords together with the melody of the song. There are millions of ways those same notes could be arranged to produce equally satisfying renditions of "Jingle Bells," so why not be free to suit yourself? It's an awful lot easier than having to learn what someone else contrived. A good analogy is to compare it with dancing. Which would be easier: to dance freely with your partner on a ballroom floor or to have to follow someone else's choreography?

When songwriters put their songs on paper, ninety-nine percent of them simply write a vocal line which they call a lead (pronounced "leed") sheet. They simply write the notes of the melody and indicate the chords above it. The publisher then asks one of his hired hands to prepare a piano part from that lead sheet. As a matter of fact some of the greatest songwriters didn't know one note from another and had to get someone else to write their lead sheets!

So-called "fake" books contain only the lead sheets of songs—just the top vocal line of the sheet music. Because of the space saved by not showing the notes for the right- and left-hand piano parts, fake books can contain over a thousand different songs! You will of course be able to play your favorite songs from fake books, the result being that you will save a lot of money by not having to buy the relatively expensive sheet music. Also, there are fake books limited to special categories such as country, blues, classical themes, Broadway show tunes, the great big-band standards of the past, etc.

The point is simply this: There is nothing sacred about the printed sheet music of the familiar songs you will be playing. You have every right to play them whichever way pleases your ears within the limits of your capabilities. Just as professional artists interpret the same songs in completely different ways, there is no reason why you can't perform them in accordance with your own personal preferences.

So the basis of my method is this: You will learn how to play melodies with your right hand (if you don't already know) and how to play chords with your left hand. You will also learn how to play those chords in different ways so that you can add interest and expressiveness to your renditions; perhaps even find a style of your own.

LESSON 1

The Piano Keyboard

It would be helpful for you to know something about the construction of the piano keyboard, so I am going to assume you are seated in front of a piano and don't know one note from another. This is what you are looking at:

BLACK KEYS AND WHITE KEYS

The keyboard is a combination of black keys and white keys, the black ones forming a pattern of twos and threes, or twins and triplets, we might say. This pattern makes it easy for us to spot the various notes. For example, the white key immediately to the left of the twins is C and, following the sequence of the alphabet, the white one immediately to the left of the triplets is F.

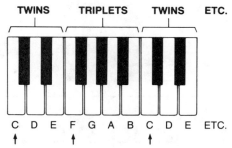

The standard keyboard has eight C's. The one in the middle (fourth one up* from the left) is called "middle C." You need only know the first seven letters of the alphabet to name the white keys, as you can see from the example above.

Although the piano keyboard looks quite large, it really consists of a series of duplications. The same notes keep repeating themselves as you go from one end of the piano to the other. The five different black keys and seven different white ones constitute all the twelve tones that have been used for centuries in the music of Western civilization as the basis for all the melodies and harmonies of all the symphonies and songs that you hear. Twelve different tones—that's all—and you can play anything by Bach, Beethoven or the Beatles.

Incidentally, none of this technical information about the construction of the piano keyboard is anything you will have to memorize or keep in mind while you are playing. It is only for your background information, but well worth a few paragraphs because it will put a lot of other important information in perspective for you. For example, if you were a foreigner inquiring about how to get from New York to Florida, my telling you about the difference in climate between the two states would not help you get there; but it would be useful to know that you shouldn't bother bringing a fur-lined overcoat with you. Similarly, knowing something about the mechanics of music will help you make subconscious judgments about the options you may have at any given time.

*When referring to the keyboard, "up" means to the right, "down" means to the left.

If you are near a piano as you read this, you might try playing the twelve notes beginning with middle C, going from left to right or vice versa. You will notice that there is no difference between the sounds made by the white keys compared to the black keys. By this I mean that if you were to close your eyes and a friend were to play various notes, you would not be able to tell which were the result of black or white keys being struck (unless you had absolute pitch, meaning that you would know exactly which notes were being sounded). Therefore, you might well ask why we need black keys as well as white.

There are basically two reasons. If the piano consisted of all white keys, it would be half-again as wide. That's because the black keys are fitted between the white ones in such a way as not to take up any additional space. Imagine trying to fit a standard eighty-eight-key piano into your living room if it consisted only of the standard-size white keys! And even if your living room could accommodate so wide a piano, imagine yourself trying to play it from one end to the other without a sliding stool!

The second reason for space-saving black keys is that it makes it possible for the average-size hand to stretch an *octave*; that is, from one C to the next one above, or one D to the next above. The interval of an octave is very important, since it enables you to *double* a particular tone. After learning to play melodies using one finger at a time with your right hand, you may find it much richer-sounding in some instances to play the melody in octaves. Also, within the comfortable span of the octave (which you usually play with your thumb and pinky) any of the eleven other tones are playable in between. This allows you to add one or more other tones that may be in keeping with the particular harmony of the tune. In discussing this now, I admit that I'm jumping ahead a bit. Therefore, if you don't quite understand the implications of adding harmonies within octaves, please don't be discouraged. All will become clear to you before you reach the end of this book.

At this point all you need to know are the designations of the white keys—C, D, E, etc. An exercise you might try is to strike white keys at random and see how quickly you can name them. You will be surprised at how soon recognition of the notes will become second nature to you.

Now we are ready to name the black keys. These actually take their names from their neighboring white ones. For example, let's look at the "twins."

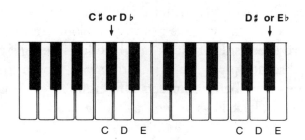

The first black key with the arrow pointing to it is between C and D. Therefore, it will take its name from the C or D on either side. Since it is higher in pitch than the white C (sharper, you might say), it can be called "C sharp." The symbol for a sharp is ♯, and so instead of spelling out the word, we simply write C♯. On the other hand, that same black key in the example above is lower in pitch than its neighboring D (flatter, you might say) and so it may be called "D flat," which is written as D♭.

The second arrow in the illustration above points to a further example of how a black note derives its designation from its surrounding neighbors. In this case we are looking at the black key between D and E, which therefore may be called D♯ or E♭. The reason why we might choose one designation instead of the other is explained in Lesson Five.

For the time being, learn to call black keys by either name, so that if I were to ask you to play C♯ or D♭ or E♭, you would have no hesitation in finding the key. Similarly, the black key between the white F and white G may be called F♯ or G♭. The black keys, therefore, are:

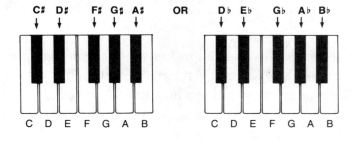

The principle behind the above designations is this: To sharp *any* note simply play the note immediately to its right; to flat *any* note, play the note immediately to its left. Therefore, if you were asked to play E♯, what would you play? Answer: the white F. What would C♭ be? Answer: the white B. In popular music for the piano, however, you will probably never encounter a C♭ or a B♯. Instead you will see a B for C♭ or a C for B♯ because it's much more direct. However, you should understand the principle involved in creating sharps and flats.

While on the subject of sharps and flats, you should know there is such a thing as a *double* sharp and a *double* flat. The symbol for the first is ×, not ♯♯, although ♭♭ is the symbol for the latter. An F double sharp (F×) is simply the note G. The rationale is that you are taking F♯ (a single sharp) and sharping it once again by moving up another half-step. Similarly, E double flat (E♭♭) is the note D. Now that you know this, file and forget it. The double sharp and double flat are almost never used in popular music, but at least you won't be shocked if you do see either of these symbols.

Once again I suggest that you try a simple exercise at the piano. Hit the black keys at random and see if you can name them quickly. At first, try thinking of them as sharps; then refer to them by their flat names. If it takes time for you to figure out the designations, don't be discouraged. When you start to play melodies, you will find that you have ample time to figure out the name of one note before playing another. Most melodies are very slow. For example, hum the first four notes of Gershwin's "I Got Rhythm," which is a fast song, relatively speaking. With your fingers, tap the four beats of those notes and you'll observe how surprisingly slow they seem to be in relation to how fast they sound when played by a band. That's because a band might include a drummer whose rat-tat-tat creates an illusion of speed that the melody alone doesn't actually have. Further, if the band also included violins playing tremolos, and clarinets playing high trills, the melody would appear to be going a hundred miles an hour. Now, here's the beautiful part: When you sit down at the piano and play the melody at *two* miles an hour, it will not be heard that way by you or anyone listening to you. Your ears will subconsciously hear all the fast orchestrations that have become associated with that song and it will sound like you are playing the notes much more quickly. (I resisted saying that you are playing at the speed of sound!)

The reason I've pointed out that tempo or speed is an illusion is that so much more of music performance is illusory. Too many people have been frightened away from trying to play because of the illusion rather than the reality. Piano playing can look and sound so much harder than it really is, just as a magic trick can appear to be impossible until you learn the surprisingly simple explanation.

INTERVALS

You now know the names of all the keys on the piano. But here is one more thing you should know about the intervals, or distances, between the keys: All adjacent keys are considered to be one half-step (or semitone or half-tone) apart. In other words, the interval between C and C♯ is a half-step, just as the interval between E and F is a half-step. The fact that C and C♯ are a white and a black key while E and F are both white has no relevance in measuring intervals: Adjacent keys of any color are a half-step apart.

Similarly, the interval between C and D is a *whole* step (or whole tone), as is the interval between E and F♯. From D to F is an interval of a tone and a half; the keys D and F♯ are *two* tones apart as are the keys C and E, and so on.

The concept of intervals is something you should know about but not something you will have to keep in the forefront of your consciousness. By understanding intervals, you will understand the logic of how the various chords are formed. But in order to play chords, you won't need to count intervals—you'll play them by sight.

Just as quickly as you can find middle C you will be able to strike a C chord, for example. That will become clear to you within a very few pages.

In closing this lesson, I would like to point out an interesting fact. If for some reason you were to stop reading this book right now and didn't see a piano for the next ten years, I would be willing to bet anything that you would be able to name every note on the keyboard. All that you have learned up to now would be fresh in your mind.

So you see, learning to play the piano is not difficult. It is made up of many simple bits of information, once learned never forgotten.

LESSON 2

Playing Melodies

This lesson is only for those who cannot read the notes on the vocal lines of songs. If you can read those notes, skip this lesson and go right to the next.

THE NOTES ON THE STAFF

Vocal lines of songs are almost always written in the *treble clef*, sometimes called the G *clef*. The G clef looks like this:

(Piano parts for the right hand are also usually written in this clef because the right hand plays higher notes than the left hand, and the treble clef conveniently designates the notes produced by the upper half of the keyboard.)

Clefs are the first symbols to appear on the musical *staff*, the staff being the name for the five lines and four spaces on which notes are written. The names for the notes that fill the spaces of the treble clef's staff spell the word "face":

The names for the notes on the *lines* result in an unpronounce-able acronym, so various phrases have been used to serve as reminders. *Every Good Boy Does Fine* is the one I grew up with, and so I recommend it to you. You won't have to think about that phrase every time you see a note on a line because recognition will soon become automatic.

As you can see, the first space on the staff represents the note F. Which F? The keyboard has seven F's but the first space on the treble clef stands for the first F above middle C.

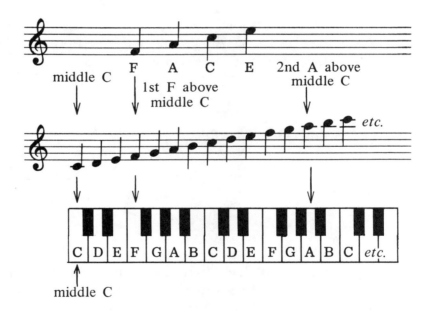

From the diagram above, you can see how the printed notes on the lines and spaces follow the piano keyboard. Also, the diagram shows how we can extend the lines and spaces both above and below the regular five-line staff in order to indicate notes that are higher and lower on the piano. Where we need a line we simply draw a small one, as in the case of middle C or the second A above middle C. Those extra lines are called *leger* lines.

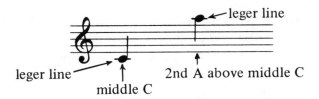

Almost all the melodies you will be playing will fall between middle C and the second F above it:

The reason is simply that the notes within that range are not only easy to read, but also best for the average human voice.

YOUR FIRST MELODY

On page 36 you will find the melody of "Silent Night" just as it might appear on the vocal line of a song book. Above it you will see a combination music-staff/piano-keyboard reminder to which you can refer if you forget the name of a particular note or its place on the keyboard. (Below it you will also see a chord reminder indicating the registers of the piano on which to play the C, F and G chords most of the time. This will be useful *after* you have learned how to play those chords in Lesson Three. Disregard the chord reminder at this time.)

There are several reasons why I chose this particular melody for your very first. To begin with, there's no doubt that you must have heard it endless times and are thoroughly familiar with it.

Secondly, it can be played exclusively on the white notes of the keyboard. In addition, it has several repetitions of note patterns within it. For example, the notes of the first two measures* (encompassing the words "Silent night") are immediately duplicated by the third and fourth measures and the notes for "Round yon Virgin Mother and Child" are the same as those for "Holy Infant so tender and mild." Finally, the melody doesn't jump around too much, most of the notes are fairly close to each other on the keyboard, and the melody covers *all* the notes from middle C to the second F above it. Thus, playing this melody is a relatively easy way for you to learn all of the white notes you are likely to come across in the vocal lines of most popular music.

You won't have to pay attention to many of the signs and symbols of musical notation that you will come across in a piece of music. However, before we learn to play "Silent Night" I would like to define a few of these symbols so you won't be confused by them. For example, the ¾ sign that you see on the staff right after the treble clef is called the *metric signature*. It means that the song is in three-quarter time (three beats to a measure), a fact that would be important only if you had never heard the melody before.

There is a sign, however, that you should be aware of only to eliminate the possibility of confusion. That sign is called a *tie* and it appears at the end of "Silent Night." It is the slightly curved line above the last word, "peace," between the two middle C's. Whenever two identical notes are tied, it means that you should not repeat the note; simply play it once and then give it the extra time your ear will tell you it deserves.

A curved line is a tie only when it connects *identical* notes. The curved line under the first two notes above the word "silent" is not a tie; the notes are different and so you play them as you would any other notes. In this case the curved line is called a *slur* and is actually meant to be observed by the vocalist. It indicates that the two notes in question are both intended for the same syllable: the "si" in "silent." The same is true for the

---

*The vertical lines that you see on the staff are called *bar lines*. They divide the music into units called *measures* or *bars*. "Silent Night" as it appears on page 36 has a total of twenty-four measures.

melody to the third word of the song, "holy," in that once again two notes provide the melody for a single syllable.

So much for ties and slurs. At least now when you come across a tie you will know not to repeat the tied note; slurs you can forget about.

You are now ready to try playing the melody of "Silent Night" (page 36). Spread the pages of this book above your keyboard and see how much fun it is to find the right notes. Be patient with yourself and you'll be amazed at how soon your fingers will follow the direction of the printed music. Use the fingers of your right hand, because you will almost always be using your left hand for the chords. However, don't concern yourself at this point with which fingers to use. The "hunt and peck" method will communicate the message just as well as the "touch type" approach.

Eventually, of course, your common sense will guide you in deciding which of your fingers to use at certain times. For example, look at the notes of the melody above the words "Virgin Mother and Child." From the first syllable "Vir" to the last word "Child" they obviously go in a downward direction, which musically means from high to low; and on the piano, high to low means right to left. Using common sense, what finger of your right hand would you begin with if you had to play notes descending from the right to the left on the keyboard, your pinky or your thumb? Your pinky, obviously.

Nevertheless, if you prefer to play the entire melody with just your thumb or your forefinger, you will still be making the right sounds. And that, after all, is the sole purpose behind the method of this book.

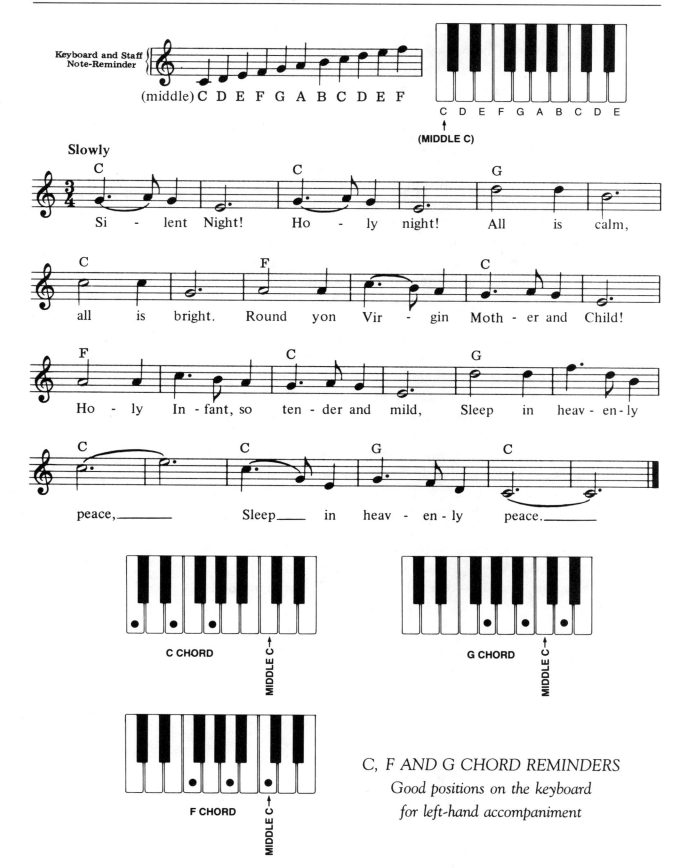

C, F AND G CHORD REMINDERS
*Good positions on the keyboard
for left-hand accompaniment*

LESSON 3

First Chords and Songs

WHAT'S IN A CHORD?

I assume that you can now play the melody of "Silent Night" reasonably well. In order to make things interesting for you as quickly as possible, I will show you how to add chords with your left hand. A *chord* is a combination of three or more tones sounded simultaneously for which the distances (called *intervals*) between the tones are based on a particular formula. (Two tones sounded simultaneously are not considered to be chords and are simply called intervals.) If you made a fist and struck four or five keys of the piano at once, you would not be creating a chord. That's because the intervals between the notes have not been arrived at through some meaningful, musical relationship. (In some forms of modern "classical" music, such fistfuls of notes, called *clusters*,* are actually considered to be chords. Not in this book, however, where we are concerned solely with traditional forms of popular music.)

*See page 59.

We will begin with simple, three-note chords, which are sometimes called *triads* to distinguish them from the four-note chords that you will be playing most of the time.

Look at the vocal line of "Silent Night" and you will see that the capital letters above it call for only three chords, C, F and G. This makes things relatively easy because those three chords are formed the same way and look alike in that they involve only the white keys on the piano.

Later you will learn the formula for creating these chords, but for now it might give you great satisfaction just to play them. Here is the C chord:

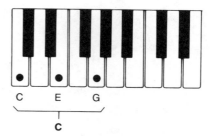

As you can see, the C chord is made up of the notes C, E and G, which you can strike simultaneously with the fingers of your left hand. The fingers usually used are the pinky, middle finger and thumb:

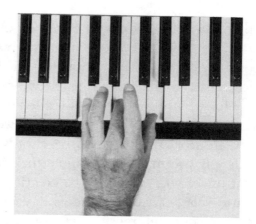

Try playing the C chord with your left hand, beginning on any C you wish. If you begin on the very lowest C of the keyboard, the sound will be somewhat muddy. When accompanying melodies, you will more than likely play the C chord on the first C below middle C for two reasons: One, it will sound good in that register of the piano and, two, it will be out of the way of the keys on which you will be playing the melody with your right hand.

At any rate, play a few different C chords so that your eye becomes accustomed to the image of it. This will happen quite soon.

The F and G chords are similar in shape to the C chord, except that they begin on the notes F and G, respectively.

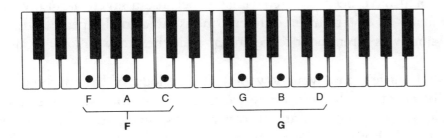

If you can readily play C chords, you will find that the F and G chords will soon be just as easy for you. As you play these chords at different points on the piano, you will begin to realize that the piano is a series of duplications, as I mentioned before. It's as though you had eight typewriters in a row, all the same, except with different-colored ribbons. You can type the same words on any of the typewriters, but they will look different. Similarly, you can get different colors from the piano, depending on which parts of it you decide to use. The point is this: Once you learn how to "type" music in one small area, you will know how to put the entire range of the instrument at your service.

Before proceeding to the next section, play the C, F and G chords sufficiently so that you can find them in no more than two to three seconds. At first you might try just using your eyes to spot the keys on the piano. Then you might simply place your fingers over the keys without depressing them. Once you find that you can get your hand in position almost immediately, you can start actually sounding the chords. The purpose behind this exercise is simply to emphasize the importance of the visual aspect of playing piano. If you can visualize what you want to play, the physical part will pose no problem.

FIRST SONGS

For the first song that you will play with both hands, turn once again to the vocal line of "Silent Night." The capital letters C, F and G that appear every so often above the staff are of course the indications for the guitar chords. Those indications, as pointed out in the first lesson, can also be used as a guide to the chords you can play with your left hand.

"Silent Night" begins with a C chord and that harmony remains in effect until the fifth measure, when a G chord is indicated. Incidentally, the C above the third measure over the word "Holy" could have been omitted. That is because a given harmony remains in effect until a different one is directed. I repeated the C simply as a reminder to beginners that they may strike it again.

I suggest that you now play the melody of "Silent Night," however slowly, and strike each chord together with the note above which it appears. In other words, when you come to the first F chord (in the ninth measure), strike it as you play the melody note (A) above the word "round." (When you play that particular F chord, a good position for it would be the one that begins on the first F below middle C.)

After you have played 'Silent Night" a few times and feel comfortable making the chord changes as indicated, you might try repeating some of the chords from time to time even though the symbol is not repeated. For example, you might repeat the F chord as you play the final note of the tenth measure; or you might repeat the G chord as you play the final note of the eighteenth measure.

Later on we will discuss numerous ways you can vary the way you play the chords. For now, limit yourself to the simple variation of playing them as seldom or frequently as you wish.

The next song I recommend for you to play is "Drink to Me Only With Thine Eyes." This calls for the same C, F and G chords you are now familiar with, but some of the changes from one to the other come more quickly than in "Silent Night."

Also, "Drink to Me" offers an opportunity to make an interesting observation about the positioning of chords, that is, which register of the piano you play them on. For example, a G chord is indicated above the word "with" in the sixth measure. If you wanted to play the G chord on the first G below middle C, your left hand would be required to play the same D as called for in the right hand melody. The least sophisticated way to solve this "problem" is simply to omit the D when you play the G chord with your left hand; the D will be provided by your right hand.

Another simple way to avoid collisions of your right and left hands (without playing the chords in the low, muddy registers of the piano) is to play the melody an octave higher than written. For example, instead of beginning "Drink to Me" on the first E above middle C, as written, begin on the *second* E above middle C.

C, F AND G CHORD REMINDERS
Good positions on the keyboard
for left-hand accompaniment

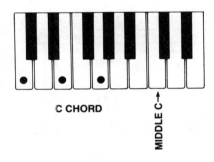

C CHORD   **MIDDLE C**

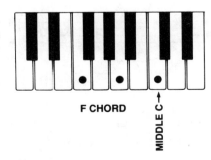

F CHORD   **MIDDLE C**

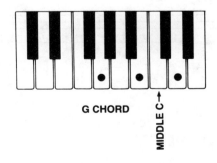

G CHORD   **MIDDLE C**

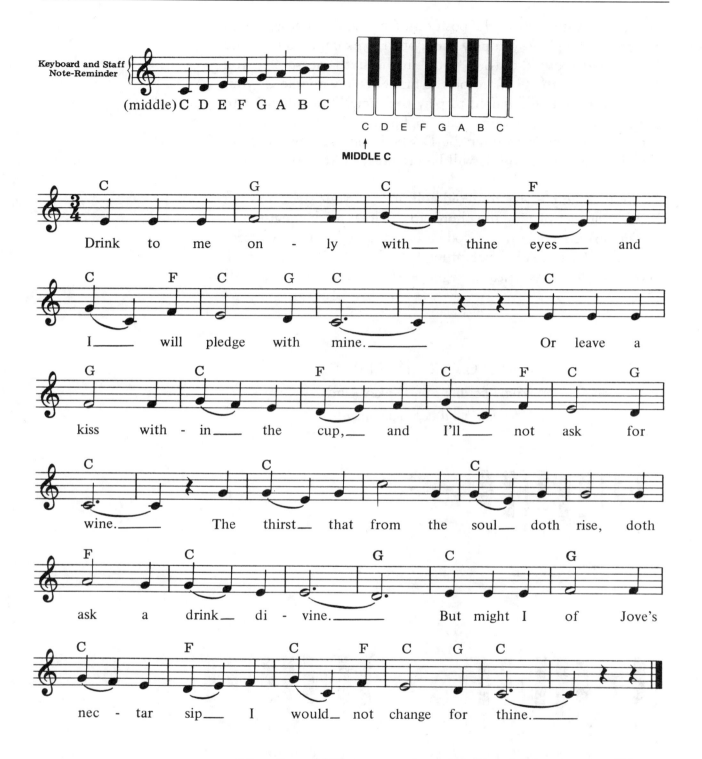

Next I would like you to play a familiar children's song, "Twin-kle, Twinkle, Little Star." This is also somewhat faster in tempo than "Silent Night" and so you get further practice in making quick changes in chords. Before you begin, observe that there are several places in the song where a G chord is called for and where the melody note is the first D above middle C. For example, a G chord is indicated in the seventh measure for the words "what you." As in the case of "Drink to Me," if you want to play the G chord in the register of the piano closest to middle C, the D of the chord in your left hand will be the same as the D of the melody for your right hand. At the present time, simply play the lower two notes of the G chord and let your right hand complete it with the D in the melody.

Also, as mentioned previously, you might try playing the melody an octave higher (beginning on the first C above middle C).

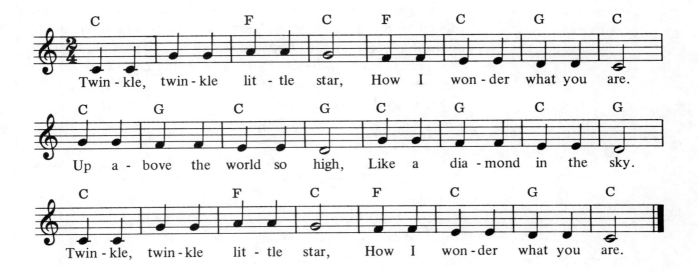

For your final "first song" I have chosen a famous marching song, "The Battle Hymn of the Republic." This will give you the opportunity to play the C, F and G chords in a steady marching beat. When you start playing your favorite contemporary pop hits, you will find that occasional repetitions of chords in a "marching" beat will be quite effective.

As a matter of fact, a steady beat can be very effective as an accompaniment to singers. For example, try this as an experiment with the chorus of "The Battle Hymn of the Republic": Play only the chords as you sing the words underneath them. The symbol / stands for a beat on which you repeat the last chord indicated.

Strike the note G on the piano to find the starting note of the melody on the first syllable of "Glory."

Before you begin, let us examine the first line of the chorus:

```
C      /    /    /    /    /    /    /
Glo  - ry,  Glory Hal-le-lu  -    jah!
```

The above indicates that you will be striking the C chord eight times as you sing "Glory, glory, Hallelujah!" The repeat symbols indicate that the first C chord will be struck as you sing the first syllable of "Glory," and the second C chord will be struck in the middle of the two syllables of that word; the third C chord coincides with the second word "glory," etc. Now try accompanying yourself as you play the chords to the chorus. Hopefully, starting the melody on G will result in a reasonably comfortable range for your voice. (Later you will learn how to start a melody on any note so that you can better accommodate yourself and others when necessary.)

As an intro, or what is often called a *vamp*, you might strike the C chord four times before beginning to sing.

```
C      /    /    /    /    /    /    /
Glo  - ry,  Glory Hal-le-lu  -    jah!

F      /    /    /    C    /    /    /
Glo  - ry,  Glory Hal-le-lu  -    jah!

C      /    /    /    /    /    /    /
Glo  - ry,  Glory Hal-le-lu  -    jah!  His

F      /    /    G    C    /    /    /
Truth  is   march-ing  on.
```

After you have played the above accompaniment with your left hand, you might try duplicating the chords with your right hand at the same time. This will be another good exercise in spotting the C, F and G chords in different registers of the piano and getting used to the different "colors" of their sound.

Another way to accompany yourself with both hands is to play only the one note that names the chord, C, F or G, with your left hand as you play the entire chord with your right. When you do this, you need not repeat the left-hand note—the *bass* note—each time you repeat the chord with your right hand. Simply hold the base note until it has to change, or until another beat seems natural to you. This is a sort of preview of things to come in your piano-playing development.

On page 46 is the lead sheet to "The Battle Hymn of the Republic" in its entirety. This time play the melody with your right hand. In other words, "Let your fingers do the walking."

C, F AND G CHORD REMINDERS
Good positions on the keyboard
for left-hand accompaniment

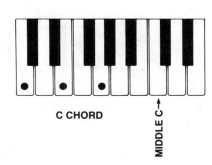

C CHORD   MIDDLE C →

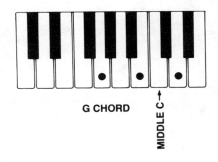

G CHORD   MIDDLE C →

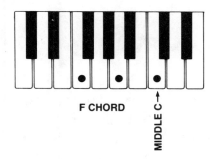

F CHORD   MIDDLE C →

Before turning to the next lesson, you might try accompanying yourself to the other songs you have learned thus far. Obviously you won't establish a marching beat for the melody of "Silent Night." More than likely you will be satisfied with only an occasional repetition of a chord. In any event, it will be a useful exercise in allowing you to express yourself in accordance with what you have learned so far. For your convenience, here are the chord-indicated lyrics to the foregoing songs. (Since you will be repeating chords at *your* option, if at all, no repeat symbols are indicated.) Strike a G on the piano to find the note on which the melody begins.

Silent Night

C
Silent Night, Holy night

G   C
All is calm, all is bright.

F   C
Round yon Virgin Mother and Child

F   C
Holy Infant so tender and mild

G   C
Sleep in heavenly peace

C   G   C
Sleep in heavenly peace

Twinkle, Twinkle, Little Star

C   F   C
Twinkle, twinkle, little star

F   C   G   C
How I wonder what you are.

C   G   C   G
Up a - bove the world so high,

C   G   C   G
Like a diamond in the sky,

C   F   C
Twinkle, twinkle, little star

G   C   G   C
How I wonder what you are.

Drink to Me Only With Thine Eyes

C   G   C   F
Drink to me only with thine eyes and

C F C   G   C
I will pledge with mine.

C   G   C   F
or leave a kiss with—in the cup—and

C F C G C
I'll not ask for wine.

       C   C   C   C
The thirst that from the soul doth rise doth

F   C   G
Ask a drink divine—.

C   G   C   F
But might I of Jove's nectar sip, I

C   F   C   G C
would not change for thine.

LESSON 4

Reading Black Keys From Music

In lesson two you learned the names of the black keys—the sharps and flats of the keyboard. Since the black keys have no names of their own but derive them from their white neighbors, they have to be called either C sharp, D sharp, F sharp, G sharp and A sharp, or D flat, E flat, G flat, A flat and B flat. (Refer to the illustration on page 26 if you need a reminder.)

Since the symbol for a sharp is ♯ and for a flat is ♭, this is the way a note is designated as a sharp or a flat on the music staff:

Once a note has been sharped or flatted, the designation applies for the rest of that measure. For example, in the following illustration the first note is the second D above middle C. Since it is in its "natural" state, that is, neither sharped nor flatted, it is called D natural. The third note is preceded by the sharp symbol, and so you would play the black note immediately to the right of the second D above middle C. The sharp symbol would also be in effect for the last D in the measure in accordance with the rules of notation.

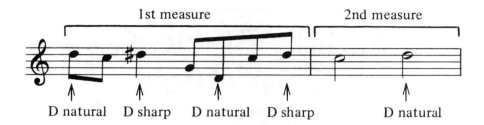

The above is a silly piece of music but it demonstrates certain principles of notation. For instance, the fifth note in the above example is a D but remains natural. Only the particular D that has been *altered* is affected by the designation throughout the given measure.

Had I wanted the last D in the first measure to revert to a natural, I would have preceded it with the symbol for a natural, which is ♮, thus:

The three symbols ♯, ♭ and ♮ are sometimes called *accidentals* because they represent departures from the usual. In fact their use in music of times past was considered accidental, hence the origin of the term.

There are times when a composer may want you to flat *all* of the B's, for example, in a particular piece. In such a case there is a shortcut that eliminates the necessity for using a flat symbol every time a B appears. The shortcut is to show the flat symbol for the B in the very first measure:

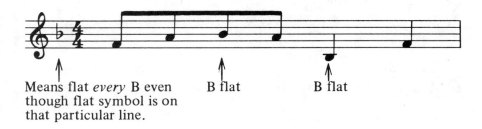

Means flat *every* B even though flat symbol is on that particular line.   B flat   B flat

The above designation is called a *key signature* because it denotes the key that a particular piece is written in. The meaning of keys in that sense will be explained in Lesson Seven. For now, the only concern is that you know how to play sharps and flats when designated in a vocal line.

Try playing the melody of "Jingle Bells" with a B flat in the key signature:

The most commonly used key signatures you will come across in popular music for piano are the following seven:

 Nothing to be sharped or flatted.

 B's are flatted.

 B's and E's are flatted.

 B's, E's and A's are flatted.

 B's, E's, A's and D's are flatted.

 F's are sharped.

 F's and C's are sharped.

As an exercise in reading the different key signatures, try playing the first eight measures of "Twinkle, Twinkle, Little Star"
using the seven different key signatures we just learned about.
(At this time disregard the chord symbols; just play the melody
with your right hand.)

LESSON 5

The Scales and Chords We Build On

You now know how to read a vocal line and how to play C, F and G chords. In order to get you started quickly in playing songs with both hands, I showed you how to play the C, F and G chords by rote rather than by principle. My purpose in starting you that way was threefold: to let you prove to yourself that you had the dexterity necessary to play chords and melodies together; to help you learn how to read the treble clef notes in a more musically satisfying way than would have been the case if you just played notes with your right hand; and to let you see for yourself how even the simplest of piano arrangements can result in beautiful sounds.

The above mission having been accomplished, it is now time to explain *why* a C chord is a C chord, why it is a *major* chord, and what common characteristics it shares with the F and G chords as well as all other major chords.

THE SCALES

To begin with, for several hundred years almost all of the music that has been the product of Western civilization has been based on the *diatonic scale*. A scale is simply an ascending or descending sequence of notes that progresses according to a particular formula. For example, a formula that calls for every note of the scale to be a half-tone apart (C, C♯, D, D♯, E, F, F♯, G, G♯, etc.) is called a *chromatic* scale. Using numbers, the chromatic scale formula might be written this way: ½, ½, ½, ½, ½, etc., the fractions representing the tonal distances, or intervals, between the notes.

CHROMATIC SCALE

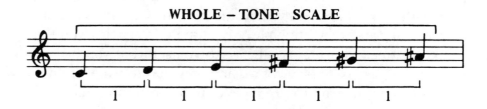

A scale based on a formula whereby every note is a whole-tone apart (C, D, E, F♯, G♯, A♯, etc., or 1, 1, 1, 1, 1, etc.) is called a *whole-tone* scale.

WHOLE – TONE SCALE

The chords we use in our "popular" music are not based on either the chromatic or the whole-tone scale so you can put them aside for now.

We base our chords on the diatonic scale. This scale has two modes, *major* and *minor*. We will concern ourselves only with the major modes in this book because your understanding of the major modes will also enable you to play any of the possible minor chords too, as you will see later.

The formula for the diatonic major scale (on which our chords are built) is based on these intervals: 1, 1, ½, 1, 1, 1, ½. No matter which key of the piano you start on, if you use that formula, the result will be a major scale. Here are examples of the C and G major scales:

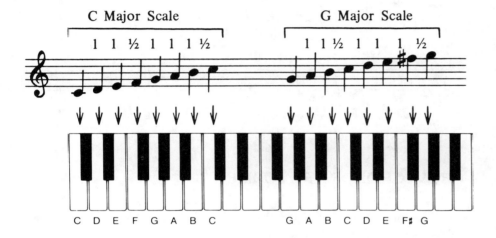

From the examples above, you will see that if you start a diatonic scale on the note C, you will be playing only natural or white notes. If you begin on the note G, you will find yourself playing an F♯ in order to conform to the diatonic formula. Actually, you will not need to practice scales or count intervals (you'll know the chords by sight just as you now can find a C chord without counting), but I suggest you try this exercise now to make sure you understand the principle involved: Play the scales of C major and G major as indicated above and observe for yourself how the 1, 1, ½, 1, 1, 1, ½ formula applies.

After playing the C and G scales, try building a diatonic scale beginning on any other note. There are twelve different notes on which you can begin and they will each have different proportions of white and black notes. I do not suggest that you try all twelve. Scales on just two or three different starting notes will be enough to demonstrate this important fact about the diatonic scale: If you listen to the notes of the scale as though they were a *melody*, they will sound like the familiar "Do, re, mi, fa, sol, la, ti, do" that we all remember from our early school days. This fact will become significant later on, when we discuss the meaning of playing in one key as opposed to another. For now, it is important only that you know how our major scale is formed.

Ex. 1   C Major

Do   Re   Mi   Fa   Sol   La   Ti   Do *etc.*

Ex. 2   D Major

Do   Re   Mi   Fa   Sol   La   Ti   Do *etc.*

HOW CHORDS ARE FORMED

The notes of the C chord (C, E and G) are the first, third and fifth notes of the C major scale.

C + E + G = The C chord (or *Triad* to distinguish it from the 4-note chords)

1st   3rd   5th

1   2   3   4   5   6   7   8

The chords we use are based on a formula that involves using every other note of the diatonic scale. Thus, the first, third and fifth notes (usually called *root*, third and fifth) of the C major scale form the C major chord, or *triad*, if you want to distinguish it from the four-note chords. (I will use the words "chord" and "triad" interchangeably hereafter.)

Some ultra-modern composers base their chords on half-tone intervals. To them a C chord might be C, C♯ and D, or an F chord F, F♯ and G. Such chords are called *clusters*, as noted at the beginning of Lesson Three. You will *never* come across those in your favorite popular songs! However, the next time you hear modern music that sounds as though the composer used his elbows on the piano to compose it, you'll know the principle behind it.

If you were to play a major scale beginning on the note F, the first, third and fifth notes would be F, A and C, constituting the F triad. Similarly, the notes of the G major triad, G, B and D, are derived from the first, third and fifth notes of the G scale. So far, our chords have all used white notes. However, if you were to play a major scale beginning on the note D, the third note would be an F♯, a black note. The same would be true if you formed an A chord or an E chord—you would find a black note in the middle. Thus, if the C, F and G chords form a trio that might be called "All White," the D, E and A chords are a trio that might be called "Middle Black."

Since there are twelve different notes on which you can build major chords, you might think it difficult to remember them. But you will find them relatively easy to form because they break down into easily recognizable patterns. Actually, they break down into four groups of three. The four groups may be called:

1. All White (C, F, and G chords)
2. Middle Black (D, E, and A chords)
3. Middle White (E♭, A♭, and D♭ chords)
4. Individual* (B B♭, and G♭ chords)

You have already played the first group of chords. Now try forming the D, E and A chords of the second group—Middle Black. Although you will find those chords just as easy to play by sight as the C, F and G chords, it is worth seeing how they arise out of the major scale:

THE D MAJOR SCALE

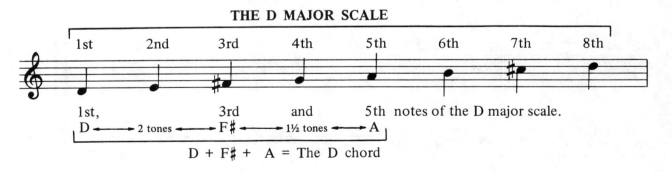

*I sometimes call these the "Mavericks."

Similarly, the E and A chords will have one black note in the middle, making the three in that group look like this:

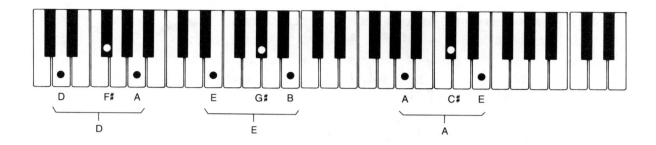

Play D, E and A chords on the piano and try to picture them as a group just as the C, F and G chords have formed a group in your mind. When you feel that you have the picture of these chords reasonably well established in your mind, play the following vocal line of "Auld Lang Syne," which has been written in such a way as to involve those chords.

The "Middle White" chords, Eb, Ab and Db, may be illustrated this way:

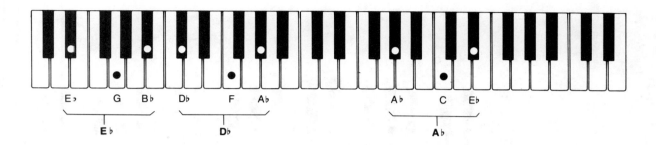

Once again, after playing this group of triads a few times you will get to know them by sight. "On Top of Old Smoky" is a good song to use as a vehicle in familiarizing yourself with those chords. Here is the vocal line:

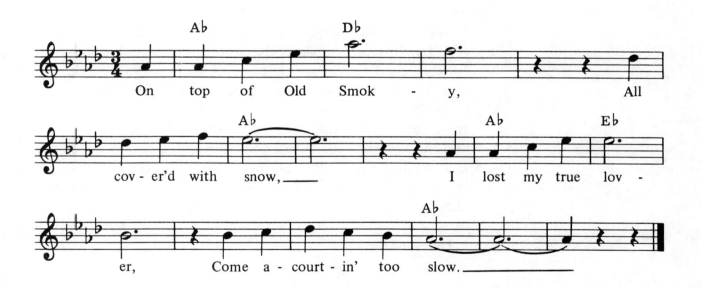

Before going to the last group of triads, it might be interesting to try the following exercise: Play the C chord and hold your fingers in place; then, still holding them in place, play the Db chord by moving each of your fingers a half-step higher. Keep progressing up the keyboard in this manner, a half-step at a time, until you reach the Gb chord. This is one of the three chords in the last group of triads that make up the "Individual" or "Maverick" group.

In playing the progression of chords in this way, you can see that the intervals between each of the notes in the chords is exactly the same. For example, the intervals that make up the C chord or the G chord are 2 and 1½, as illustrated below:

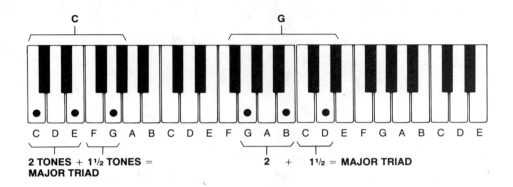

Similarly, the intervals between the D, F♯ and A of the D chord are 2 tones between the D and the F♯ and another 1½ between the F♯ and the A. The intervals of 2 plus 1½ will form a major chord on every one of the twelve different keys of the piano keyboard. Up to now you have formed chords on nine of those twelve keys, the three All White, the three Middle Black and the three Middle White. The remaining keys, G♭, B♭ and B, constitute the "Individual" or "Maverick" group, so-called because each of the chords on those notes is unique in appearance, although the 2-tone, 1½-tone formula applies.

Here are the chords:

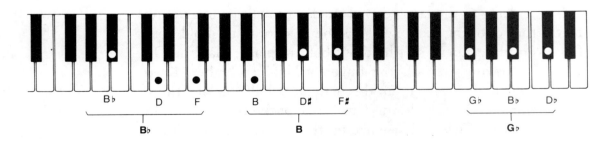

The Bb chord (one black followed by two white keys) and the B chord (one white followed by two black keys) are unique in their particular patterns; and the Gb chord is the only all-black chord of the twelve.

Play the following progression of chords a few times: Bb, B, C; Bb, B, C; Bb, B, C, etc. This will impress you with the fact that the Bb, B and C chords are exactly alike as far as their intervals are concerned, even though they don't resemble each other.

Similarly, play the progression of F, Gb and G chords and you will see the logic of the construction of the Gb chord in relation to its all-white neighbors, F and G.

Of the three triads in the Individual group, the Bb will probably be the most frequently used in popular music. Here is the vocal line of "Yankee Doodle," which will not only get you started in using the Bb chord, but will help familiarize you with melodies written in a three-flat key signature.

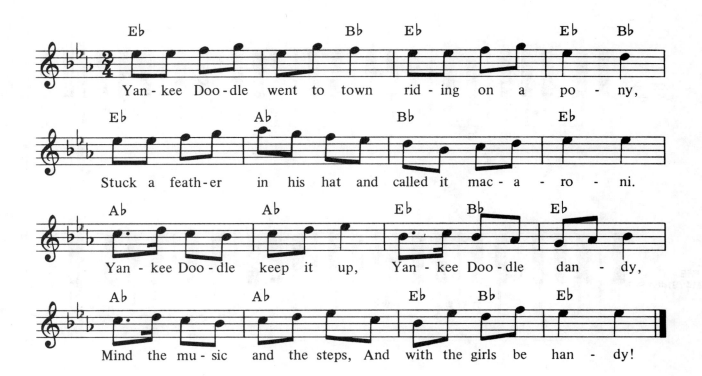

Here are illustrations of all twelve major triads. This will serve as a quick and easy reference for you while playing any of the songs in the first eight lessons of this book:

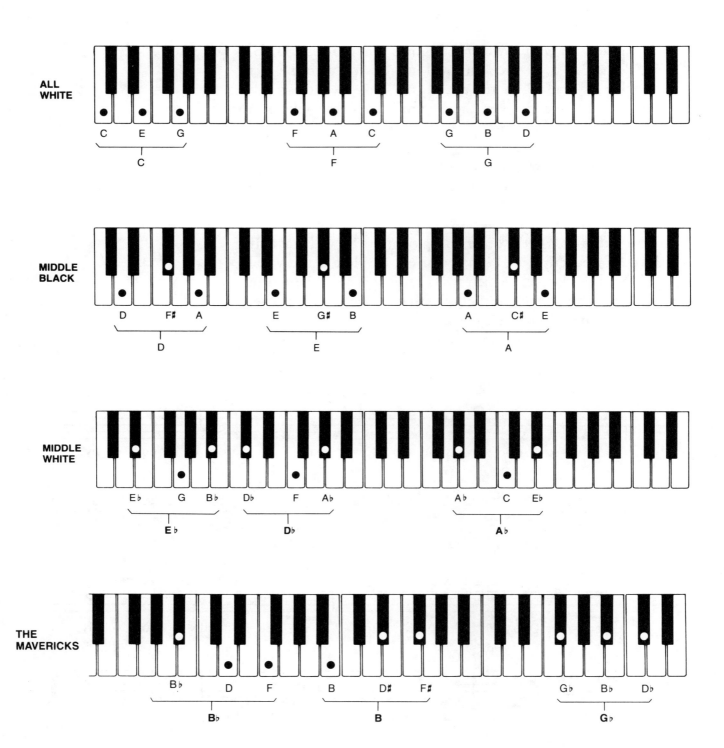

SHARP OR FLAT?

As indicated earlier, the note E♭ may also be called D♯. It follows therefore that the chord starting on that note may be called D♯ as well. However, you will rarely, if ever, come across that designation because it is much more complicated to "spell" musically. Here's why:

These are the notes of the E♭ major scale:

To form this same scale on the basis of sharps rather than flats (as above), would result in this:

You can see that it becomes necessary to call for an F *double sharp** as well as a C *double* sharp in order to follow the musical alphabet consistently in constructing the D♯ major scale. Although there *is* such an animal as F double sharp, you won't find it in the kind of popular music that this book is concerned with. It simply makes life a lot easier to base this scale on E♭ as opposed to D♯. Just imagine what the key signature would look like if we used D♯ as the basis!

*See page 27.

LESSON 6

The Meaning of Tonality

Whenever you sing or play a major scale (the one we know of as Do, re, mi, fa, sol, la, ti, do), an interesting thing happens: the starting note of the scale becomes its focal point, or home plate, so to speak. For example, if you play the C scale, the note C will become to your ears the note of ultimate resolution; it will seem to have a gravitational force that pulls all the other notes of the scale to it.

Play the C scale on the piano a few times and then play C by itself two or three times. After doing this, play the note B. Observe how the sound of that note wants to lead you to C in order to create a feeling of resolution. If you just played the B without resolving it, you might have a sense of waiting for the other shoe to drop. (I say "might" because we all vary in our sensitivity to tonal relationships. If your feelings of tension and resolution don't conform to the foregoing, please don't be dismayed. You are still fully capable of learning to play your favorite songs and understanding the patterns involved. Just follow along with the rest of us!)

With C still established in your mind as home plate strike a D. Once again you will probably feel that C is exercising its gravitational force, trying to pull you back to it in order to release the tension. The other notes in the scale will create different degrees of tension with respect to getting back to C. In my own case I find that the notes G, B and D leave me with the strongest feeling of wanting to get back "home," whereas the remaining notes A, F and E diminish in that order in their demand for resolution.

On page 53 the melody of "Twinkle, Twinkle, Little Star" has been written in seven different keys, that is, it has been structured on seven different major scales. In the first example it is based on the C major scale, a scale that has no sharps or flats. Therefore the key signature bears no sharp or flat symbols.

In the second example, "Twinkle, Twinkle, Little Star" is in the key of F. The scale of F has a B♭ in it (in order to conform to the diatonic major scale formula) and so the key signature contains a B♭.

When you play this melody in the various keys shown on page 53, note how readily your ear accepts each different "home plate" note. That note is commonly called the *tonic** since it defines the particular tonality involved. Thus C is the *tonic* in the first example, F in the second, B♭ in the third, etc.

The melody of "Twinkle, Twinkle, Little Star" happens to start on the tonic of whichever key it is written in. Thus in the last example on page 53 it begins on D, and the key signature of two sharps reflects the fact that it *is* in the key of D. However, melodies do not necessarily begin on their keynotes. "Drink to Me," when played in the key of C, as shown on page 37, begins on E, the third note of the C scale. This means that if it were written in the key of F (*transposed* to F), it would start on A, the third note in the F scale.

To *transpose* means to play the same piece of music, be it a song or a symphony, in a different key. When you play "Twinkle, Twinkle, Little Star" in C, as in the first example on page 48,

*or *root* when referred to in the context of being the *root* of a chord, as shown on page 58.

and then play it in D as in the last, you are transposing that melody. The intervals between the individual notes of the melody will remain the same no matter which of the twelve possible notes you start on. The chorus of "The Battle Hymn of the Republic" will always begin on the fifth note of the scale of whatever key you play it in. On page 41 it is written in the key of C and it therefore starts on G. If you were to transpose it to the key of E♭ it would start on the fifth note of the E♭ scale, namely B♭.

To sum up this lesson, when we say that a piece of music is in the key of C we mean that its individual notes and chords will be built on the notes of the C major scale. Since there are no sharps or flats in the C major scale, the key signature will bear no sharp or flat symbols. However, that does not mean that no sharps or flats will ever be called for. For example, look at the fourth measure of the "Star Spangled Banner," written below in the key of C:

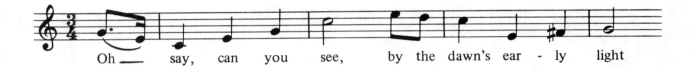

Although there is no F♯ in the C scale, that does not preclude its being used in the fourth measure of the melody. The F♯ will be heard by the ear as it *relates* to the C scale, since the tonality of the tune clearly defines C as its home plate.

Last in this summary is a word about transposition. Why play something in one key as opposed to another? There are many reasons, but two will suffice for present purposes:

1. If the music involves singing, one key may be better suited to one's vocal range than another. (Check this by singing "Twinkle, Twinkle, Little Star" in the different keys shown on page 53.)

2. In instrumental music, too, some keys are more appropriate than others for an instrument's particular register. (This you will be able to demonstrate to yourself after you have begun playing "by ear," the principles of which you will shortly learn.)

LESSON 7

Altering Major Triads

Now that you know how to form major triads, you are ready to learn the four basic ways they can be altered.

MINOR CHORDS

The first is to change them from major to minor. Simply lower the middle note (the third) by a half-step (flatting it, in other words). For example, C, E, G are the notes for the C major triad. Therefore, by flatting the middle note, E, we get C, Eb, G, and those notes constitute the C *minor* triad. The symbol for C minor is simply "Cm," which is the way you will find it above the melodies in vocal lines and lead sheets.

Here are some illustrations of minor triads (next to their major counterparts):

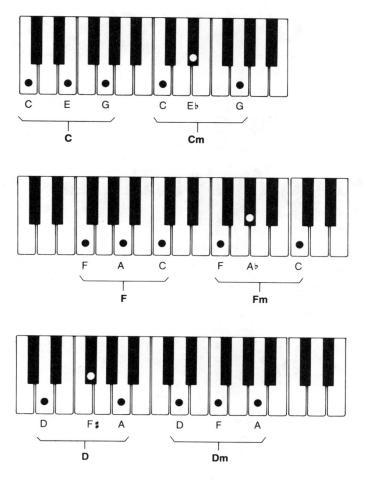

Note that the D major triad becomes an all-white chord when you make it minor. By lowering the middle F♯ of the major triad, we arrive at the natural F—a white note.

Once again let me reassure you that you will not have any problems trying to remember the minor chords. You will soon learn to spot them by sight without having to form their major versions first. Here are the notes of some of the most frequently used minor triads. Play them over several times and familiarize yourself with their sound and appearance. You might find it help-ful to play the major version first.

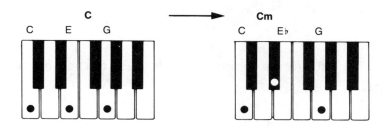

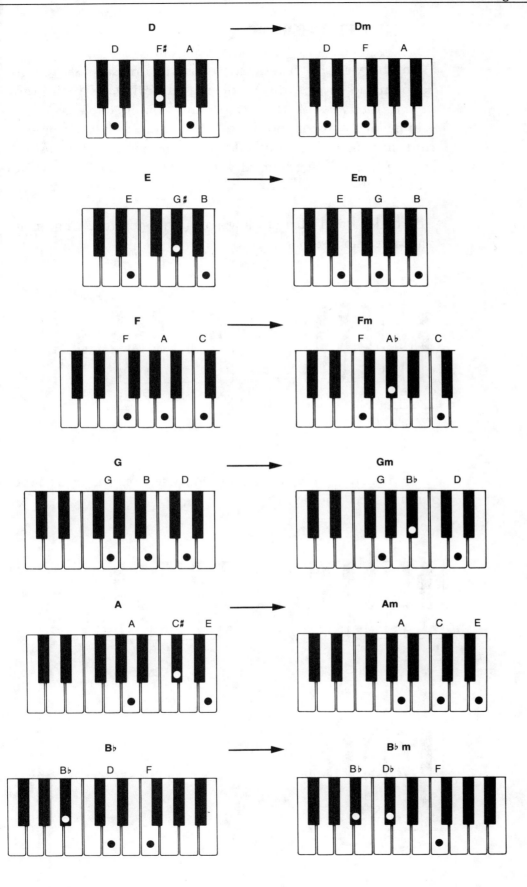

DIMINISHED CHORDS

Another way of altering major triads is to form *diminished* chords. As the name implies, this involves a narrowing, or diminishing, of the intervals of the major and minor chords. Whereas in making a major chord into a minor one you lower only the third, in making a diminished chord you lower the fifth as well. Thus, a C diminished chord would be C, E♭ *and* G♭; a G diminished chord would be G, B♭ *and* D♭.

Both third and fifth are lowered a half-step to change major triads to *diminished* ones.

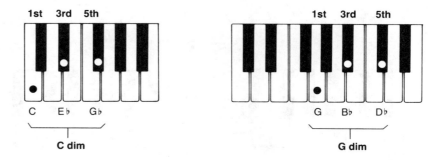

As an exercise, play chords in sequence from major to minor to diminished, thus:

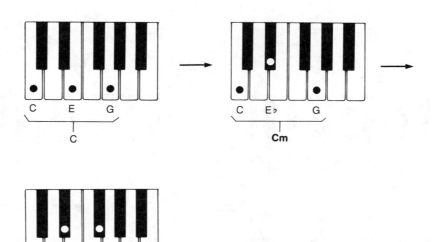

After going through the above sequence with the C chord a few times, try the same with the following:

F → Fm → Fdim
G → Gm → Gdim
D → Dm → Ddim
E → Em → Edim
A → Am → Adim

The following melody of "America" has been harmonized to include minor as well as diminished chords. I purposely added "extra" chords to give you practice in finding them on the keyboard. Actually, this melody would sound just as good if played with only one chord on the first beat of nearly every measure. There are four places in this song where you will play an E♭ diminished triad immediately followed by an E diminished triad. Once you find the first of these, you can simply hold your fingers in position and move each up by a half-step. You might try playing those chords in succession a few times before beginning to play the entire song.

AUGMENTED AND SUSPENDED CHORDS

Besides altering major chords to become minor and diminished, there are two other alterations that are sometimes used. They are the *augmented* and *suspended* versions, which are easily formed when you start with the major triad.

To augment the C triad, for example, you simply raise the fifth by a half-step. C augmented is therefore C, E and G♯; G augmented would be G, B and D♯, thus:

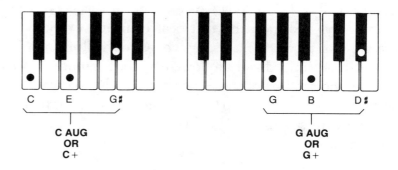

As the name implies, when you augment a chord you are *extending* it somewhat. Old-fashioned songs are more apt to call for augmented chords than contemporary music. Nevertheless, you will find them quite effective when they are called for.

Suspended chords, on the other hand, are one of the most frequently used alterations in modern music. You will find yourself suspending chords at your own option in order to give added interest to the harmony.

To suspend a chord, simply raise the third by a half-step. Thus C suspended is C, F, G; G suspended is G, C, D. In effect you are raising the third note of the major scale to the fourth. That is why the symbol for a suspended chord may appear as "Csus4" as well as the simple "Csus."

Suspending a chord actually creates a sense of tension which is resolved when the suspense is over, that is, when the raised third is lowered to its normal position.

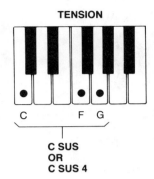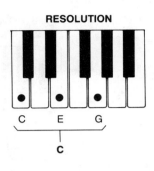

Although suspensions are much more effective when applied to four-note chords, there are times when they sound good when used with triads. For example, in "Silent Night" on page 31, a G triad is called for in the seventeenth measure above the word "sleep." Try suspending the G chord on that word and resolve it on the first syllable of "heavenly" in the next measure. Instead of repeating the outer notes* of the chord (G and D) simply release the C and play the B.

Similarly, on page 42, suspending the G chord in the second measure of "Drink to Me" will be quite effective. Its resolution should take place within that measure on the second syllable of "only." The same suspension can be used wherever the melody repeats itself as on the word "kiss" in the tenth measure.

You now know how to form major, minor, diminished, augmented and suspended triads. Before beginning to learn the four-note chords, which will complete your ability to harmonize melodies, play the C, F and G chords in the aforementioned five versions: major, minor, diminished, augmented and suspended. That should be sufficient for you to establish the principles behind the formation of each of those versions.

INVERSIONS

Up to now you have been playing chords in what is called their *root position*. The root of a C major or C minor chord is C, the

*Sometimes called the *frame* or *shell*.

first note. When you play root, third and fifth in that sequence, from the bottom up, you are in root position.

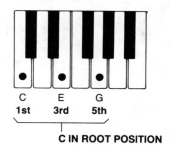

In producing the harmony or sound of a C major chord you are not limited to that one particular sequence: as long as you play *any* combination of C, E and G, you will be signaling the sound of a C major chord loud and clear. Thus, if instead of playing C, E, G, you play E, G, C or G, C, E, you are playing an inversion of the C chord, but a C chord is a C chord is a C chord!

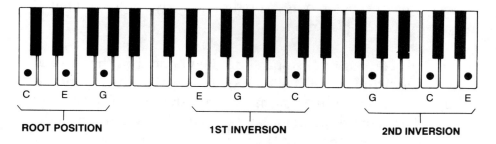

From the illustrations above you can see that a three-note chord can be played three different ways. Inversions allow you to make subtle, qualitative changes in the sounds of chords; they also allow you to move conveniently from one chord to another. For example, in moving from a C chord to an F chord, you already have a finger on the note C that is common to both chords. All you need do is move the E and G up to F and A and, presto!, you have gone from the C to the F chord.

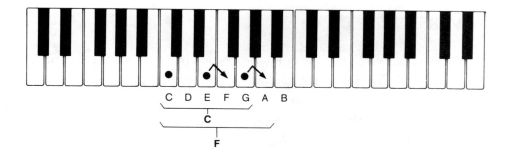

Suppose you were playing an inversion of the C chord with middle C on top and you wanted to move to a G chord but didn't want your left hand to go above middle C. This is how you would facilitate that change:

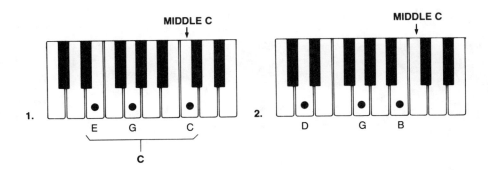

In the example above you have moved from the first inversion of the C chord to the second inversion of the G chord. However, when you actually play inversions and move conveniently from chord to chord, you won't be aware of whether you are playing first, second or *any* inversions; your eye will spot the notes you want just as you now can spot middle C on the piano.

The important thing for you to remember is that you have certain options available when you put the notes of a chord together. You are not locked in to building chords on their roots; you can build them on any of their notes in accordance with what is comfortable and produces the sound that pleases you best.

There are times when the composer or arranger of a piece may want an inversion of a chord rather than its root position. There is a simple way to specify this in the chord symbol. For example, if the second inversion of the C chord is desired (G, C and E instead of C, E and G), the symbol would be C/G. The G after the slash means that you should play the C chord with G as the bottom, or bass note, instead of C. Thus, if you come across G/B, it means play the G chord with a B as the bass note: B, D, G.

Such inversions are rarely indicated for the triads but are used more commonly for the four-note chords. Triads are usually inverted for logistical reasons. But inversions of four-note chords can produce exciting musical effects, as you will soon learn.

LESSON 8

Four-Note Chords

Four-note chords are almost as easy to learn as three-note chords, but their names and the ways in which they are formed are sometimes confusing. So I don't want it to come as a shock when you discover that the rules for forming three-note chords may in some cases not apply to four-note chords. Don't think that perhaps you're not grasping some important principle because the name of a certain chord doesn't seem to make sense. *You* are right: it's the system that's inconsistent.

Remember that it's only the *nomenclature* that's complicated, not the chords themselves. You will find them easy to play and musically satisfying. At first you may find it somewhat awkward to put your fingers on them comfortably. However, if you give yourself ten minutes or so to get the *feel* of a certain chord, you will find it just as easy to play as the C, G or F triads.

SIXTH CHORDS

The first and simplest group of four-note chords are the *sixth* chords. They are formed by simply adding the sixth note of the scale to the major or minor triad.

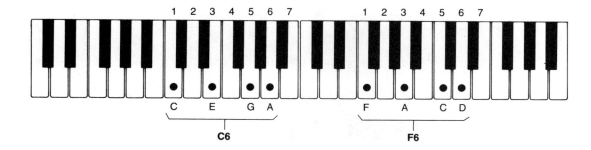

From the example above you can see that a C sixth, the symbol for which is "C6," is made up of the notes C, E, G and A, A being the sixth note in the scale of C. The sixth note in the scale of F is D, and so an F6 is F, A, C and D. A simple way to find the sixth note is to play the note that is one whole-tone above the fifth. For example, if you see G, B and D as the notes of the G chord when you look at the piano, you can see that E is the note that is a full tone above the fifth, which is D. Here is a picture of that chord with the fingering I recommend for all sixth chords in root position.

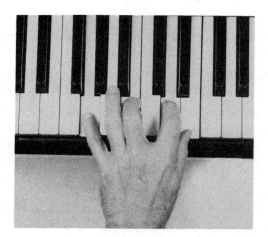

The fingering above—pinky, middle finger, forefinger and thumb—is undoubtedly the fingering you will find most comfortable for all the four-note chords, even, for the most part, when you invert them.

Because the fourth finger is generally the weakest, it isn't used much except when you are playing a note adjacent to the one you are playing with your pinky; and that rarely happens when playing chords with your left hand.

The only change we make with sixth chords is from major to minor. We don't diminish or augment them in popular music. Fortunately, the rule for turning major sixth chords into minors is the same as for triads: Lower the third by a half step.

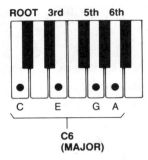

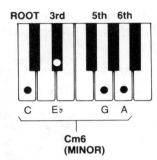

Play the triads you know and then add the note that will transform them into sixth chords. I suggest the following sequences:

$$
\begin{array}{lll}
\text{C} & \rightarrow \text{C6} & \rightarrow \text{Cm6} \\
\text{F} & \rightarrow \text{F6} & \rightarrow \text{Fm6} \\
\text{G} & \rightarrow \text{G6} & \rightarrow \text{Gm6} \\
\text{E}\flat & \rightarrow \text{E}\flat\text{6} & \rightarrow \text{E}\flat\text{m6} \\
\text{B}\flat & \rightarrow \text{B}\flat\text{6} & \rightarrow \text{B}\flat\text{m6} \\
\text{B} & \rightarrow \text{B6} & \rightarrow \text{Bm6}
\end{array}
$$

If you can do the six groups above with reasonable facility (even if you have to pause and think for thirty seconds), you have mastered the principle of forming sixth chords, and that's all that counts. Speed will come before you know it.

Don't be discouraged if facility doesn't come right away. All it takes is practice. You may find that you grasp certain things quickly and then seem to reach a plateau where you don't feel as though you're making progress. Then, you suddenly gain an insight and start making progress until you reach another plateau. Plateaus are to be expected and should not discourage you. As long as you understand the words in this book, there is no doubt that you will ultimately be able to apply them to playing the songs of your choosing. This I know from long experience in teaching this method.

SEVENTH CHORDS

The most important four-note chords are the sevenths. In fact, most contemporary pianists will play a C major seventh, for example, when a plain C is the symbol in the lead sheet of a contemporary song. The major seventh chord produces a modernistic effect and therefore would be inappropriate for songs such as "Silent Night" or "The Battle Hymn." However, you will find its effect highly gratifying when you play "Raindrops Keep Fallin' on My Head" and other modern songs.

Major sevenths To form a C major seventh, you add the seventh note in the scale to the C triad you already know, thus:

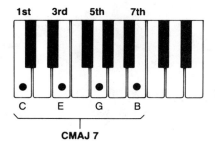

Since C6 stands for C major sixth, you might logically expect C7 to stand for C major seventh. Unfortunately, we have run into a case of inconsistent nomenclature, because C7 stands for C *dominant* seventh, a chord that differs from the major seventh chord. Therefore, in order to specify a *major* seventh chord, the abbreviation "maj" must be used in the symbol as shown above.

As far as the fingering of the seventh chords is concerned, I recommend pinky, middle finger, forefinger and thumb, as noted previously for sixth chords. If at first you find it difficult to play the four notes cleanly, that is, without accidentally pressing extra notes down, do not worry about it. As long as you know what you are aiming for, you will very soon hit your mark perfectly. The difficulty with beginners is not an inability to stretch the distance, or lack of dexterity; it is simply the feeling of trepidation that causes tension in the fingers. But once you relax, and that will happen after anywhere between ten minutes and ten hours at most, it's clear sailing for all chords from then on.

Observe that the seventh note in major seventh chords is always the note that is a half-step below the root-note of the chord. Thus the seventh note in a Dmaj7 would be C♯; in a Gmaj7 it would be F♯.

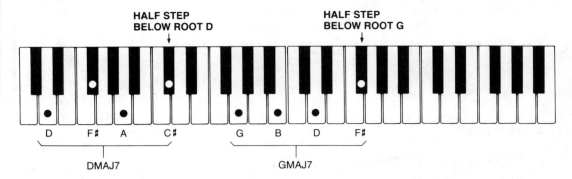

The C♯ and F♯ in the example above are easy to spot because they are just below the root notes of the chords.

As an interesting exercise in using both a sixth and a seventh chord, I suggest that you play just the first two measures of "Raindrops Keep Fallin' on my Head" (pp. 86–87). Play the simple F triad on the first beat of the first measure. When you get to the first syllable of "fallin'" in the first measure, play an F6 chord (even though not indicated) by adding the note D to the F triad. Then on the first beat of the second measure, play the Fmaj7 as indicated above the word "head." If you take your left-hand thumb off the D in the F6 chord and move it up a full step to the E, you will have an Fmaj7.

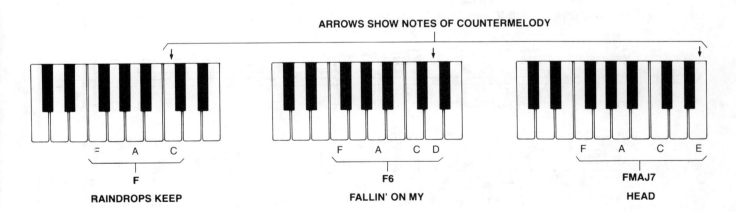

By playing the F triad, F6 and Fmaj7 in root position as indicated above, the top notes of the chords will move from C to D to E, producing an interesting *countermelody*. (As the name implies, a countermelody is a series of notes that create the effect of a secondary melody when played together with the primary one.) This countermelody will be enhanced if you return to the F6 chord in the middle of the second measure.

From The 20th Century-Fox Film
"BUTCH CASSIDY AND THE SUNDANCE KID"

RAINDROPS KEEP FALLIN' ON MY HEAD

Lyric by
HAL DAVID

Music by
BURT BACHARACH

Although piano stylings will be covered in a later chapter, I wanted you to have a preview of things to come, along with learning the various F chords. Also, your ability to play the first two measures of "Raindrops" as indicated should give you a justifiable boost in self-confidence. You've come a long way since "Twinkle, Twinkle, Little Star."

Dominant sevenths We come now to the dominant seventh chord, and I believe it is worth explaining the origin of its name. The explanation will give you some useful background information which you will appreciate having later on. (Most of the following technical language is "file and forget" material; but read it anyway.)

Each note of the major scale has a name which is meant to describe its relationship to the keynote or root, which in technical language is called the *tonic*. The second note is called the *supertonic*, the third the *mediant*, the fourth the *subdominant*, etc., as shown in the example below.

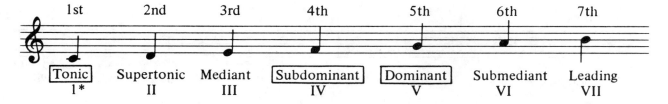

1st	2nd	3rd	4th	5th	6th	7th
Tonic	Supertonic	Mediant	Subdominant	Dominant	Submediant	Leading
1*	II	III	IV	V	VI	VII

*Roman numerals are often used for referring to the chords built on the different degrees of the scale. For example, the first four chords of "Drink to Me" on page 42 are C, G, C, F, which can be described as the I, V, I and IV chords or as the tonic, subdominant, tonic and dominant. Roman numerals are particularly useful in avoiding references to the terms supertonic or submediant, which are awkward.

I have boxed the most important degrees of the scale, the first, fourth and fifth notes, which are the *tonic, subdominant* and *dominant*. Chords built on those notes of the scale have been the basis of almost all the music written long before Beethoven and well after the Beatles. More will be said about this in the lesson on playing by ear. For the present it is only necessary to define the fifth note of the scale as the dominant, and to learn how the dominant seventh is built on it.

In the scale of C, the fifth note, G, is the dominant scale degree. Therefore the dominant seventh chord for the scale of C will be G seventh, symbolized simply as "G7," as pointed out before. Since dominant sevenths have to be built on the notes of the scale to which they belong (or we wouldn't define them as *dominant*), the notes of the G dominant seventh chord must come from the C scale. (After all, we are treating G as the fifth note in the key of C, not the first in the key of G or the second in the key of F, for example.) In order for it to be defined as a seventh chord, the interval between its outer notes must be a seventh. Here are the notes of the C scale from which we will construct the dominant seventh chord:

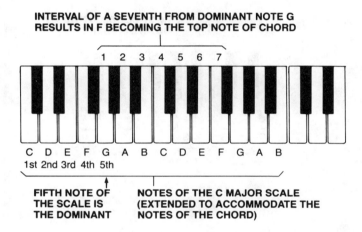

The simplest way to find the notes of any dominant seventh chord is to think of the top note as being a whole-tone below the root note. Thus a D7 would have C as its seventh; C7 would require a B♭.

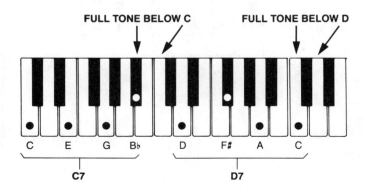

Another way to find dominant sevenths is to compare them with major sevenths. You simply play the upper note a half-step lower.

GMaj7 = G,B,D,F#
G7   = G,B,D,F,   ½ step below F#

CMaj7 = C,E,G,B
C7   = C,E,G,Bb   ½ step below B

To help you grow accustomed to the faces of the two seventh chords you have learned thus far, do the following in sequence: Play a triad and double the root note with your thumb an octave higher, thus:

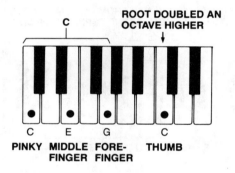

Now move your thumb down a half step to form the C major seventh chord, thus:

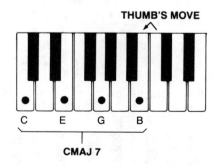

Move your thumb down another half-step, to form the dominant seventh, thus:

Do the above progression from the doubled-root chord to the dominant seventh with the following list of seven:

C	→	Cmaj7	→	C7
F	→	Fmaj7	→	F7
B♭	→	B♭maj7	→	B♭7
E♭	→	E♭maj7	→	E♭7
G	→	Gmaj7	→	G7
D	→	Dmaj7	→	D7
A	→	Amaj7	→	A7

After you have done the above progressions a few times, you will probably find that some are easier to remember than others. If that is the case, don't worry about those that may cause you to pause and think an extra thirty seconds. When you start to play songs of your own choosing, you will find that when you play the "troublesome" chords in that context, you will soon spot them at sight just as quickly as any of the easy triads. That is because their beautiful sounds in your favorite songs will have a profound effect on your memory.

PLAYING MAJOR AND DOMINANT SEVENTHS

At this point in my private lessons, I authorize some of my students to do a little cheating and rush ahead. I tell them they can try to play their favorite songs, with the following provisos:

A. If diminished, augmented, minor or suspended sevenths are called for, ignore the seventh note and play only the triad based on the root. Thus if Cdim7 is specified, play a simple C diminished triad; if Am7 is specified, play a simple A minor triad.

B. Do the same as above in the case of ninth chords, such as C9 or Cm9, etc.

C. Ignore any symbols not explained thus far and just hold your fingers on the previous chord; chances are that the "strange" symbol is calling for a transitional chord that can just as well be omitted.

D. Under no circumstances try to guess the meaning of the new symbols, because nomenclature in music is not necessarily consistent, as you already know, and you may jump to the wrong conclusions.

Now, if you want to jump ahead a little, and if you promise to observe the ground rules above, do so. At least you will be gaining practice in playing many of the chords you have already learned. Also, if you did not know how to read notes before reading this book, it will be helpful for you to read different melodies in different key signatures.

ALTERING SEVENTHS

The best way to learn the remaining seventh chords is to think of them in terms of the *dominant* seventh. For example, to form a C minor seventh you lower the E of the *dominant* seventh to an E♭, just as you did when going from a C major to a C minor triad.

Perhaps you expected to form a minor seventh chord by lowering the third of a *major* seventh. Although musical logic breaks down again, there is a bright side to all this: if you use the *dominant* seventh as your base, the rule for forming minor, augmented and suspended sevenths is the same as that which applied to the triads. (The *diminished* seventh chord is the only exception, but its construction makes sense; you won't have any problem with it.)

Using the dominant seventh as the base, here is how the various sevenths are formed:

MINOR SEVENTHS—THREE EXAMPLES

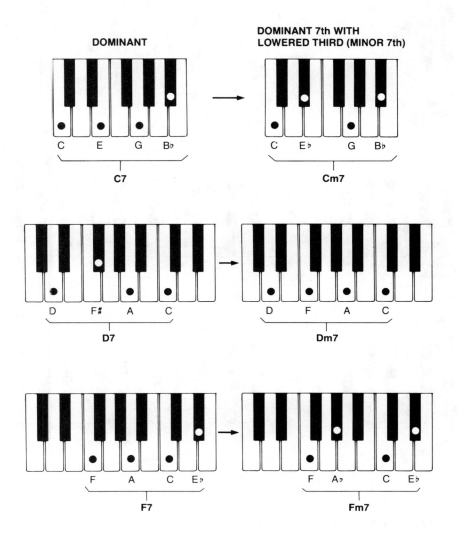

Familiarize yourself with the following minor sevenths in addition to the above:

Em7 (E, G, B, D)
Gm7 (G, B♭, D, F)
Am7 (A, C, E, G)
Bm7 (B, D, F♯, A)
B♭m7 (B♭, D♭, F, A♭)

AUGMENTED SEVENTHS—THREE EXAMPLES

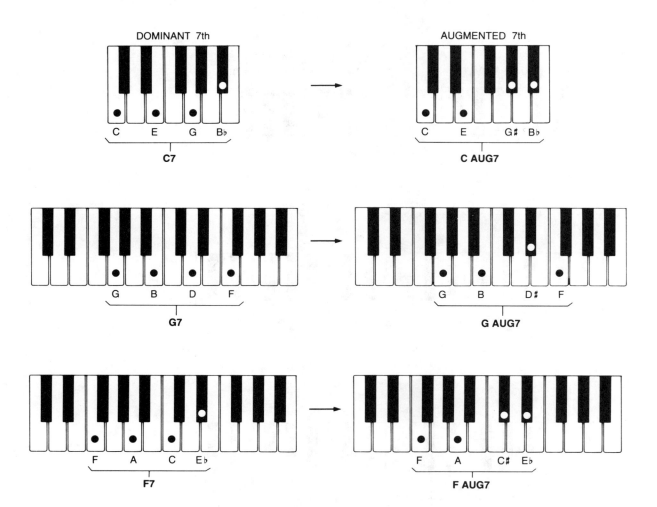

Augmented sevenths are infrequently used in modern songs. Depending upon how well you feel you have grasped the *principle* behind their construction, you can decide how many different ones you want to play.

SUSPENDED SEVENTHS—THREE EXAMPLES

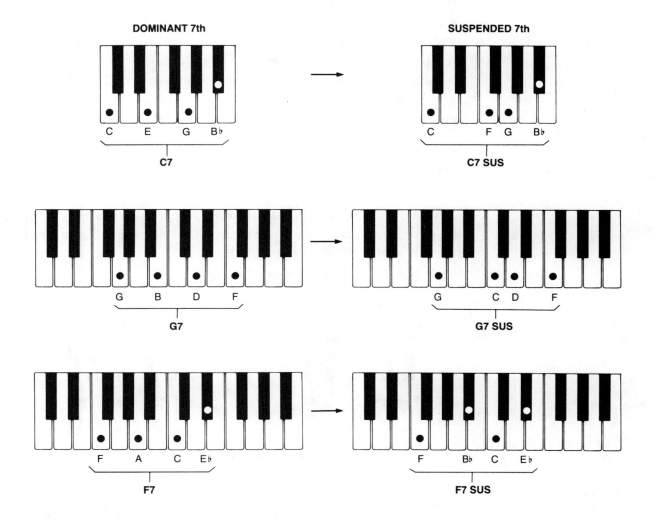

Suspended sevenths are used quite frequently and you will probably use them even when they are not designated. Therefore, it is advisable to learn the following:

D7sus (D, G, A, C)
Eb 7sus (Eb, Ab, Bb, Db)
Bb 7sus (Bb, Eb, F, Ab)

An easy way to spot suspended sevenths is to visualize the dominant seventh first. Then simply raise the third to the fourth.

Another useful exercise when you play suspended sevenths is to resolve them to their dominant forms by sounding only the third with your middle finger while holding the other three notes in place. The reason for doing this is threefold: You will be getting practice in moving one finger (the third in this case) while holding the others in position; you will be reinforcing the relationship in your mind between these closely related chords, both as to sight as well as sound; you will be better prepared to make the resolutions when they are indicated in the music you will play.

DIMINISHED SEVENTHS—THREE EXAMPLES

We come now to the last and least frequently used sevenths, the diminished sevenths. Once again it is best to use the dominant seventh as the basis for forming them. In that case all you do is lower the third, fifth *and* seventh notes, thus:

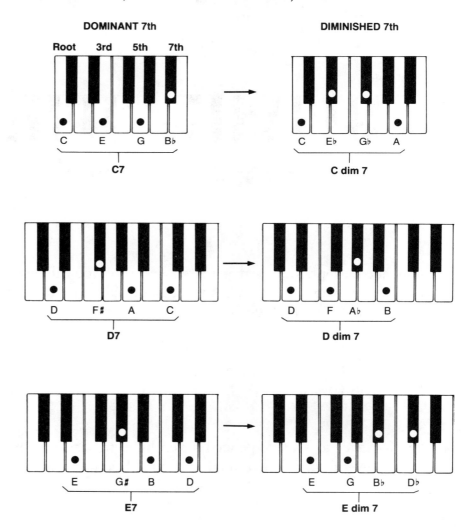

Interesting sidelight: The above three are the only diminished sevenths you need to be familiar with. The nine other diminished sevenths consist of the same notes as in any one of the chords shown above. For example, a Gdim7 would be G, B♭, D♭ and E, the same notes used in Edim7 but inverted; an E♭dim7 is made up of the same notes as those found in a Cdim7, namely E♭, G♭, A and C, again inverted. Each of the three diminished sevenths illustrated above can be played four different ways (root position followed by three different inversions), and that gives us the twelve that are possible. It is the only type of chord that can have four different root names, using the same four notes in each chord, and continue to be a diminished seventh in each case!

The following illustrations will make the meaning of all this much clearer, particularly if you play them yourself.

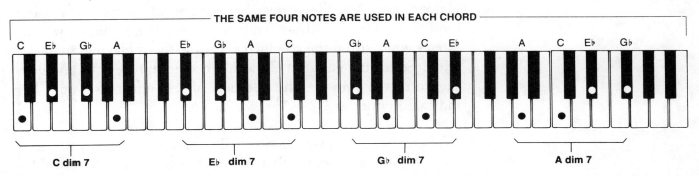

Although these three chords are inversions of Cdim7, they have *root* names of their own, unlike the C7 chord inversions shown below. The interesting result is that diminished seventh chords soon become relatively easy to spot on the keyboard.

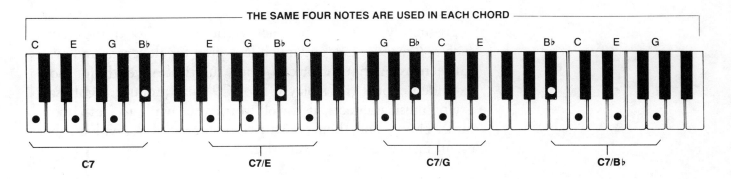

These inversions do not have simple root names of their own as is the case with the inversions of diminished seventh chords shown above.

There are two important alterations that may be specified in the symbols for seventh chords. The most frequently used one is for a flatted fifth. Thus C7♭5 or C7-5 means you play C, E, G♭, B♭ instead of C, E, G, B♭. Flatting the fifths in dominant seventh chords produces a very modern sound and you might try doing that even when the music does not specify it.

The other alteration involves adding a note "outside" of the regular notes of the chord. For example, if you were playing a C7 chord with your left hand and the melody involved C's, E's and/or G's, the harmony would still be that of a C dominant seventh because the melody is simply duplicating some of the notes of the chord. However, if you are required to play an A♭ in the melody, the harmony has been changed. As far as the piano is concerned, if only the C7 symbol appeared above the melody note A♭, the correct harmony would automatically be produced. However, those symbols are meant for guitars, which often merely strum the specified chords without playing the melodies. So for the guitar, a C7 would not be sufficient to produce the correct harmony. The addition of the note A♭ would be indicated either as C7+A♭ or C7addA♭.

Therefore, as a pianist, you will find that you can disregard some of the alterations that are specified. You will probably be effecting them by simply playing the melody along with the "straight" chord, e.g., a plain C7 instead of C7+A or C7+A♭.

NINTHS AND OTHER EXTENDED CHORDS

Frequently, you will come across the symbols for ninth chords such as Cmaj9 or C9, and much less often for elevenths and even thirteenths. Although you can simply substitute sevenths for those extended chords (i.e., play C7 for C9) and produce highly satisfying musical effects, it is well worth your while to learn about ninth chords and their construction since it will involve other useful facts about music notation.

In the first place, a *ninth* refers to the interval of a ninth that results from playing the first and ninth notes of the scale simultaneously. This is an easy stretch for most hands, as you will probably find by playing a C with the pinky of your left hand and playing the D that is eight notes higher with your thumb:

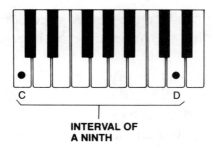

**INTERVAL OF
A NINTH**

Theoretically, these are the notes that constitute a C major ninth and a C dominant ninth chord: C, E, G, B, D, and C, E, G, B♭, D, respectively. I say "theoretically" because I don't know many pianists who can play all those notes comfortably with one hand. However, by playing extra notes with the right hand, in addition to the melody, the full chord is easily played.

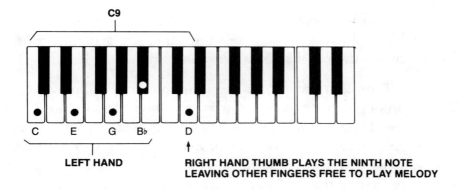

LEFT HAND

**RIGHT HAND THUMB PLAYS THE NINTH NOTE
LEAVING OTHER FINGERS FREE TO PLAY MELODY**

There are times when the ninth note (for example, the note D in a C9 chord) is a part of the melody. In that case a C7 symbol would actually result in a C9 chord. But you will almost always see a C9 symbol in the music anyway. The reason, as previously mentioned, is that those symbols are meant for guitars or banjoes, which mostly strum the chords without playing the notes of the melody. Therefore, it makes a significant difference to those instruments as to whether a C7 or C9 is indicated. Also, those instruments can play elevenths and thirteenths, not to speak of ninths, as easily as a pianist can play triads. (When you strum the open strings of a guitar with your right hand you are producing an interval of two octaves—a fifteenth. Try doing *that* on the piano—with one hand!)

The fact that you will be playing notes of the melody with your right hand while you play the chords with your left means that if you play only sevenths in place of the higher-number chords, you will probably produce the desired effect anyway. The melody notes will be adding the necessary *extra* intervals.

Once you understand the principles of forming seventh chords, the ninths are easy. All you do is add the ninth note in the scale to the seventh chord and you have the corresponding ninth chord. For example, when you add a D to a C7 you have a C9; when you add a D to a Cm7 you have a Cm9.

The most common alteration of ninth chords occurs with the dominant ninth chord and involves the flatting of the ninth note. For example, C, E, G, B♭, D♭ is a C ninth in which the ninth note, D, has been flatted. This is usually symbolized as C7♭9 or C7−9. (The ♭9 or −9 is what tells you it is a ninth chord despite the C7 in the symbol.)

Ninth chords are too large to be played comfortably by one hand of average size. Therefore, they are generally split up between the two hands as previously shown.

"Autumn Leaves" is a beautiful song that will provide you with an opportunity to review what you have already learned. It is an excellent example of how dominant seventh chords yearn to be resolved by their tonics. For example, observe how satisfying it is to play the G chords after the tension created by the D7's preceding them. Also, the B7 chords are just as satisfyingly resolved by the E minor chords that follow in every instance. Going from G to D in the first case or B to E in the second is a V–I progression. The fact that in the latter instance the chord of resolution is *minor* rather than *major* doesn't matter. The note B is the dominant degree in the E scale, major *or* minor, and therefore a dominant seventh on that degree longs for the resolution provided by an E chord. (See Circle of Fifths, page 111.)

Two other points are worth noting with respect to this song. First, the B7−9 symbol near the end of the song above the word "miss" should be regarded as simply B7. This is true because the C in the melody provides the flatted ninth note. As pointed out on page 99 the melody often provides those notes that are needed to be added to seventh chords to make them ninths, or to ninth chords to make them elevenths, etc.

The second point has to do with the first and second endings as designated above the last two measures. If you have any ques-

AUTUMN LEAVES
(Les Feuilles Mortes)

English Lyric by
JOHNNY MERCER

French Lyric by
JACQUES PREVERT

Music by
JOSEPH KOSMA

tion about them, the explanation of the first and second endings in the appendix, page 138, should make their meaning perfectly clear.

I believe you will enjoy playing this song as much as you will benefit from doing so.

VOICING

The order in which the notes of a chord are played is called its *voicing*. The voicing of the C9 chord shown on page 91 is called *closed* because the individual notes are as close together as they can possibly be in root position. Inversions such as E, G, Bb, C, D or G, Bb, C, D, E, for the C9 chord, are also examples of closed voicings. Most musicians prefer *open* voicings played by both hands as follows:

OPEN VOICINGS OF C9

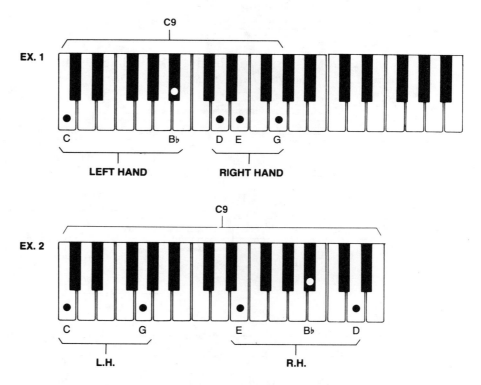

Often some notes of the ninth chord may be omitted. For example, if the G or E were omitted in the above illustration, the ear would still hear the remaining notes as a C9.

At this point you know every chord you need to know in order to play "Raindrops Keep Fallin' on My Head." You may even omit some of the chords which are completed by the melody, such as the D9 in the fifth measure, above the word "seems." The effect of the ninth will be established by the note E in the melody right after that word.

When we get to numbers above the ninths such as elevenths and thirteenths, we are in the realm of polychords. These, as the name suggests, are two different chords played simultaneously. For example, a C11 is really a C chord with a Bb chord on top.

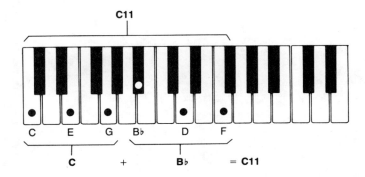

The symbols you will see for elevenths and thirteenths are mainly for guitarists, not for pianists. As pointed out before, the chances are that when you play the notes of the melody you will be adding the eleventh and thirteenth notes to the seventh or ninth chord you are using as a substitute. In any event, the principle of forming elevenths and thirteenths is the same as that for forming ninths. Just as you added the ninth note to a seventh chord to form the corresponding ninth chord (major, minor, etc.), you add the eleventh note to the ninth chord to form the corresponding eleventh chord, etc.

You will rarely come across symbols for elevenths and thirteenths. If you do, substitute seventh chords and you will undoubtedly produce a beautiful sound. Also, if any alterations are specified, such as C11addAb, add the note Ab to the seventh chord if it is not in the melody and you will have the essential tones you need. Sometimes music arrangers get carried away with their expertise and end up complicating matters unduly. Let your ear and plain common sense be your guide. Never be intimidated by an awesome symbol.

LESSON 9

Jazz Piano Styles

There are many styles of playing that sound really great, as you must know if you have listened to Teddy Wilson, Oscar Peterson, Dorothy Donnegan, Marion McPartland, George Shearing, etc. Each musician can play the same song in a unique way without letting the song lose its identity. Although your goal may not be to become one of the great performing artists, learning some different styles of playing can certainly increase your enjoyment and make your efforts sound more professional and interesting.

SWING BASS

Instead of playing a particular chord straight, that is, striking all the notes at once and holding it, you can *swing* it. Using the F chord as an example, and assuming we have the usual four beats to a measure, you can play the root note, the F, by itself in the lower register of the piano on the first beat, then "swing" your arm up the keyboard and play the full chord (F, A, C) on the second beat; "swing" down again, but this time play the fifth by itself (in this case the C immediately below the low F) on the third beat, and then swing back to the same full chord for the fourth beat.

Usually you alternate the root and the fifth in the bass only when playing the tonic and dominant chords. For example, "Raindrops" is in the key of F. Therefore, F and C7 are the tonic and dominant chords: alternate root and fifth on those. In other cases, use your judgment as to whether you should just repeat the root in the bass or play the fifth. In many cases there will be a quick chord change, so you will only have time to play the root and chord once. For example, in the sixth measure of the chorus of "Raindrops," the chords are Am7 for the first two beats and D7 for the third and fourth. In swing bass style, you would play a low A followed by the Am7 chord for the first two beats and then a low D followed by the D7 chord for the next two. (No time for the low fifths here.)

There are other things you can do to add interest to the swing bass style. You can play inversions of the chord rather than stick to the root position. You can also play the first-beat bass note in octaves rather than as a single note.

Try swinging different chords, alternating their roots and fifths in the bass. This will familiarize you with the best positions to use so that you don't get in the way of your right hand when you play a particular chord. You will also learn what sounds to expect from the different registers of the piano.

When a song is in ¾ time, such as a waltz, you would play the root on the first beat and then play the chord on the second *and* third beats. When there is no chord change after three beats, you can play the fifth in the bass instead of repeating the root on the next first beat. Thus, you would be playing *root*, chord, chord, *fifth*, chord, chord, *root*, chord, chord for the *one*, two, three, *one*, two, three rhythm.

BLOCK CHORD

This is a style that George Shearing uses quite effectively. He also has a unique sense of harmony, and so the chord substitutions he makes (B7 for G7, for example) add great interest to his playing.

The idea behind the block chord style is to play the melody in octaves, using one finger of each hand, and to play the notes of the chords *within* those octaves, using the fingers of the right hand. For example, if you wanted to play "Silent Night" in block chord style, reading the melody as shown on page 36, the four notes of the first two measures would be played this way:

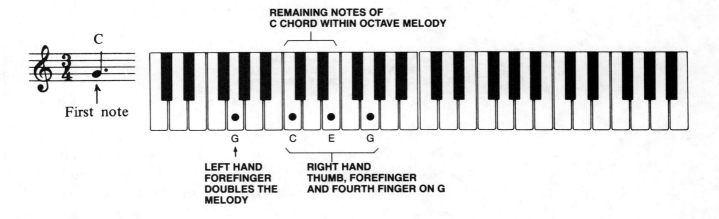

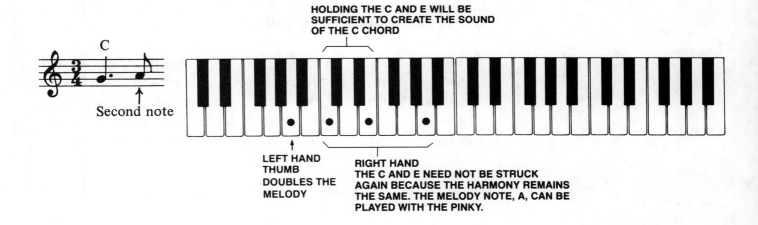

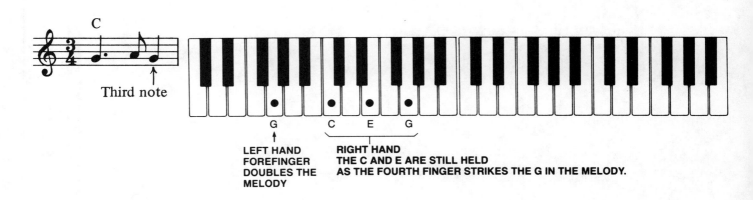

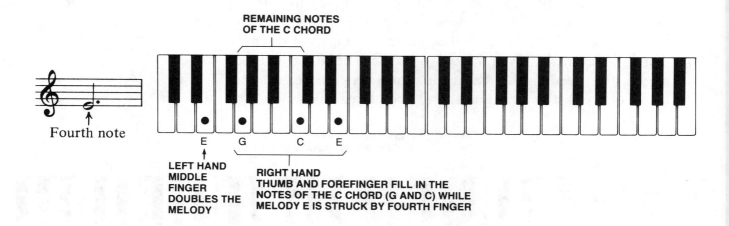

Fourth note

REMAINING NOTES
OF THE C CHORD

LEFT HAND
MIDDLE
FINGER
DOUBLES THE
MELODY

RIGHT HAND
THUMB AND FOREFINGER FILL IN THE
NOTES OF THE C CHORD (G AND C) WHILE
MELODY E IS STRUCK BY FOURTH FINGER

When playing block chord style, you should be careful not to fill in too many notes of the harmony, lest you produce "muddy" sounds. For example, if a Gdim7 is indicated, you can probably omit at least one of the notes without losing the desired harmony. The ear will often hear notes that aren't struck because those that are will provide *overtones* sufficient to provide the missing tones. So keep in mind that playing *fewer* notes in block chord style will often provide a better quality of sound, and will allow for greater agility of the fingers.

One of the great benefits of the block chord style is that it forces you to find the notes of chords within a specific framework. This increases your ability to spot the various inversions. This style also emphasizes the fact that the piano is a series of duplications: you have everything you need within the confines of an octave!

ARPEGGIATION

An *arpeggio* is the sounding of the notes of a chord in succession rather than simultaneously. Here are examples of the notes of F chords in the form of arpeggios:

Although I illustrate them in treble clef, arpeggios in popular music are usually played in lower registers of the piano when accompanying melodies. The above are examples of *closed* positions since they follow the closed positions of the chords. The first of the examples above creates a Mozartian effect when played with the left hand an octave lower against a melody in the right. Try the first few measures of "Raindrops" that way.

More often than not pianists use wide-open arpeggios that extend over several octaves. Again, using treble clef for ease of illustration, here is a wide-open arpeggio of a C chord:

The above would sound good when played two octaves lower as an accompaniment to "Silent Night." Since "Silent Night" has three beats to a bar, use only the first six notes of the arpeggio above (two notes to each beat) for the first measure and repeat them for the second, etc., until the harmony changes. At that point, arpeggiate the change (in this case a G chord) in similar fashion.

HARMONIC

The flatting of fifths in seventh chords is an important characteristic of contemporary styling. Also, it is often good to let the flatted fifth be the bottom note of the chord. Thus a C7♭5 would be played as G♭, B♭, C and E rather than C, E, G♭ and B♭.

As noted before, the dominant seventh chord gets its name as a result of being built on the dominant note, or fifth degree, of the scale. Dominant sevenths create a feeling of tension that begs to be resolved by the sound of its tonic chord. Thus, our ears want to hear an F chord after hearing a C7 (because C is the dominant note of the F scale), or a C chord after hearing a G7. (Imaginative composers find interesting ways to prolong the tension rather than resolve it immediately. They often do this by surprising us with a harmony we didn't expect, thereby creating a memorable effect.)

A modern way to play the tonic chord is to play it in the form of a major seventh. For example, instead of going to a simple C, E and G after playing a G7, contemporary pianists will play C, E, G, B—the tonic as a major seventh. As indicated above, it is common practice these days to play the dominant seventh chord with its flatted fifth in the bass. If we use the key of C as an example, going from the dominant seventh with a flatted fifth in the bass to the tonic would mean going from D♭, F, G and B to C, E, G and B. This is a comfortable progression in that the pinky and middle finger of the left hand on the D♭ and F slide down a semitone to the C and E, while the forefinger and thumb on the G's and B's restrike their notes. Try this progression in the seven different keys shown on page 47.

Circle of fifths As previously noted, the dominant seventh chord creates a longing in our ears for the sound of its tonic. To demonstrate this to yourself, play a G7 four or five times in succession. Having established that sound in your mind you will undoubtedly find that when you play a C chord—even just the note C—you will have relieved the tension created by the sound of the seventh chord. This dominant-to-tonic progression, or V7–I as normally labeled,* has been the harmonic foundation of the music of western civilization for centuries.

An interesting extension of that dominant-to-tonic progression was to treat the tonic as a new dominant, thereby creating a new feeling of tension requiring new resolution. In other words, instead of playing the tonic C chord after a G7, you would play a C7 chord. That C7 chord creates a new tension which now seeks resolution through the sound of an F chord. If in turn that F chord is played as an F7, the progression wants to continue. As you can see, if we continue turning tonics into dominant sevenths (G7 to C7 to F7 to B♭7, etc.) we can form a complete circle of dominant sevenths called a *circle of fifths.* It is so called because if you begin on any note and ascend by fifths (for example, C to G to D to A, etc.) or descend by fifths (for example, C to F to B♭ to E♭, etc.) you will pass through all the twelve possible tones, ending up where you began.

This circle is always depicted as follows, and can be used as a reminder of how many sharps or flats there are in each key:

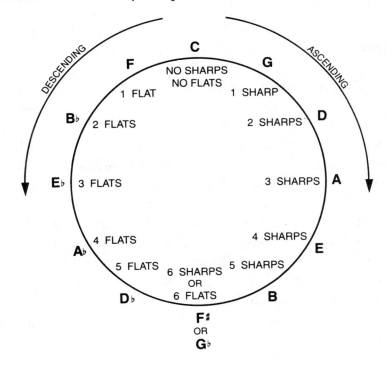

*See page 88.

The most important thing to bear in mind is that this circle is normally applied in a *counterclockwise* direction as far as chord progressions are concerned. This will be demonstrated shortly, with respect to its use, in "Raindrops Keep Fallin' on My Head" and "Moon River."

When composers harmonize songs they don't necessarily go through the entire circle. A string of four or five chords in the progression is generally about all you will find in a given song. In the key of C, for example, you will often come across an A7 followed by a D7, then a G7 leading to the tonic C.

Also, the circle of fifths can be applied in an interesting way by including *minor* sevenths as well as dominant sevenths. Thus in the key of F you might find an Am7 (instead of A7) followed by a D7, which in turn is followed by a Gm7 (instead of G7), after which comes the regular C7 leading to the tonic F. As a matter of fact, that is the progression you will find in "Raindrops Keep Fallin' on My Head" (shown on page 86).

Look at the sixth measure (counting from where the lyrics start) above the word "fit" and you'll see the symbol Am7. This is followed by D7 to Gm7 to C7sus (a little intriguing suspense before the regular C7) and home to F. Thus the progression of root notes—A to D to G to C to F—follows the circle of fifths, as diagrammed above, and in a counterclockwise direction.

There are times when you may not immediately recognize the use of the circle because a transitional chord has been inserted to add interest. (The C7sus chord between the Gm7 and the C7 in "Raindrops" is just such an example.) However, to paraphrase the words of "Raindrops," it won't be long before harmonic awareness steps up to greet you! When that happens you will find yourself adding harmonic interest to songs by using the appropriate parts of the circle at your own option. Instead of playing a D7 immediately, for example, you might try preceding it with an A7 or Am7, and perhaps succeeding it with a G7 or Gm7 if not already specified. The most important thing is to be aware of the fact that the circle exists and is so much a part of the music we hear. You will then take advantage of the opportunities to use it.

This is the perfect time for you to play "Moon River" (p. 114), a song that uses the circle as beautifully and originally as any song I know. Look at the fourteenth measure (counting from where the lyric begins) over the word "goin'" and you'll see the symbol F♯m7−5. That F♯ chord is the start of a circle that takes us to where the words "Two drifters" repeat the opening melody. The letters of the chords are F♯, B, E, A, D, G and C. If you refer to the diagram on page 102 you'll see that those chord-letters represent more than half of the complete circle, counter-clockwise of course.

In addition to having created an absolutely beautiful melody, Henry Mancini makes use of the IV chord in an ingenious way. In the key of C, that is the F chord, and it occurs in the third measure on the word "wider." (I play an F7 there as opposed to a simple F.) What "makes" the song for me is the use of the F chord against the B in the melody—a musical, Mancini miracle!

MOON RIVER

Words by
JOHNNY MERCER

Music by
HENRY MANCINI

Jazz musicians practice various chords by playing them through the circle of fifths. In this way they can instantly play whatever chord they want in any key. For example, here are two modern voicings of a chord that can be used to represent a C7 or C9:

FIRST VOICING

C

↑

LEFT HAND PINKY PLAYS THIS
C IN THE BASS ON ONE BEAT AND
THEN MOVES UP TO PLAY THE REST OF THE CHORD
ON THE NEXT BEAT.

E   A ↑   D

Bb

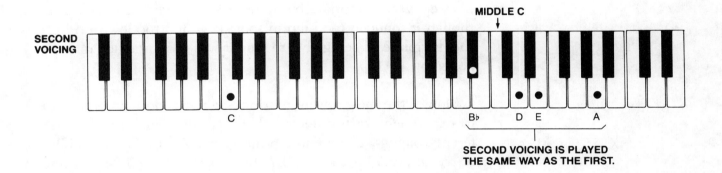

MIDDLE C
↓

SECOND VOICING

C

Bb   D   E   A

SECOND VOICING IS PLAYED
THE SAME WAY AS THE FIRST.

The choice of whether to use the first or second voicing will depend on the logistics of the moment: where the two hands are, which notes are being played by the right hand, which register is best for different keys.

When jazz pianists practice the voicings above, they will run them through the circle of fifths. Thus, after playing the first voicing of the C chord above, they will hit an F in the bass and play the remaining A, D, Eb and G. After the F they will go to Bb, etc.

Should you ever discover a chord of your own, so to speak, that you like very much, I suggest that you run it through the circle so that you will be able to use it in whatever key you happen to be. For instance, a jazz teacher I met recently showed me this chord as a substitute for C7 or C9:

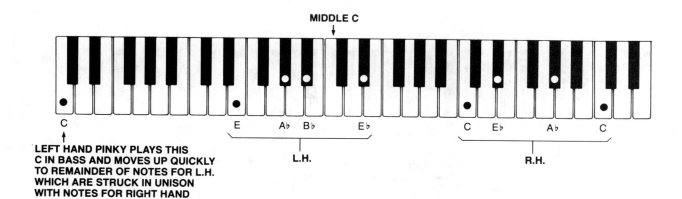

MIDDLE C

E   Ab Bb   Eb   C Eb   Ab   C

LEFT HAND PINKY PLAYS THIS C IN BASS AND MOVES UP QUICKLY TO REMAINDER OF NOTES FOR L.H. WHICH ARE STRUCK IN UNISON WITH NOTES FOR RIGHT HAND

L.H.   R.H.

I liked the voicing above so much that I made sure I could use it whenever appropriate by running it through the circle. Even though it sounded too high in some keys and too low in others, the discipline of being able to play it was good practice in transposition.

One of the most rewarding things you can do harmonically is to experiment with different chord substitutions as well as different voicings. If the music bears a symbol for a C7, try a Gb7, or try an Am6 instead of a B7. Eventually, you will learn something about your individual preferences, not to speak of how much fun you will have while getting a "college education" in harmony.

RHYTHMIC

You could almost fill the pages of a book this size just by giving a short definition of the numerous rhythmic forms of jazz that have developed since ragtime emerged in the early 1900s. Dixieland, swing, rhythm and blues, be-bop, rock 'n' roll, not to mention soft rock, hard rock, punk rock, new wave and reggae— these are just a few. There are also the early blues, boogie-woogie, different forms of country as well as cool jazz, hot jazz and disco.

One of the most important styles is that made so popular by the Beatles, namely, soft rock (or ballad rock as some call it).

This style is often adapted to accommodate the great songs of the '30s and '40s by Gershwin, Rodgers and Porter, for example, as well as most of today's pop music. It is called *soft* to distinguish it from *hard* rock, which involves the use of various electronic devices as well as extremely amplified electric guitars. The lyrics of hard rock songs can be as raucous as the instrumentation, as opposed to the somewhat tender, plaintive words to such songs as "Yesterday" or "Michelle" by the Beatles.

The most important characteristic of rock music is its rhythmic pattern. Just as the *one*-two-three, *one*-two-three beats of a waltz identify the form as surely as antlers identify reindeer, the persistent pulsating of eighth notes in 4/4 time tells you you're hearing rock, whether or not you know what an eighth note is.

The other rhythmic feature that is essential to rock has to do with syncopation. Although the two rhythmic features just mentioned are difficult to explain in prose, away from a piano, it is not impossible. If you proceed step by step as follows, I believe you will not only understand the meaning of rock but will be able to play it yourself.

To begin with, if you say the word "baby" four times at your normal talking speed, you will have articulated eight syllables which can stand for the eight eighth* notes to each measure. This can be illustrated as follows:

The numbers show where the four beats (accents) of each measure occur naturally. I use the word "naturally" because it is characteristic of rock to shift the accented notes to an offbeat position rather than keep their normal on-the-beat position. To demonstrate this to yourself, go back to the rhythmic setting of the word "baby" above and clap your hands eight times for the eighth notes while tapping your foot four times to represent the natural beats. Thus you will be tapping your foot on only the first syllable of "baby" but clapping on both. When you can do that with ease, refer to the illustration of syncopation below.

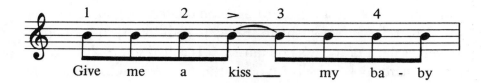

Tap exactly the same way for the above as in the first example, except that in clapping, just keep your palms together on the fifth note which is tied and therefore not sounded. Also, when you clap on the fourth note, give it a little accent as indicated by the accent mark above it. To help you do this more easily, you can say, "Give me a *kiss*, my baby" with an accent on the word "kiss" which comes on an offbeat note. Syncopation arises when you stress a weak beat, one not normally accented. That's why the above is an example of syncopation.

Following is an *un*syncopated version of "Give me a kiss, my baby":

In the example above, no weak beat is being accented nor is any strong beat being anticipated as is the third beat in the previous example. By letting the word "Give" take up two eighth notes instead of one, the word "kiss" is delayed enough to make it fall on the third, naturally accented beat.

Syncopation does not necessarily have to occur in every measure of a rock song. As a matter of fact several measures can go by without it, but sooner or later it is almost bound to occur because of the nature of rock and the words that go with it.

Now that you know something about the construction of rock music you can start to play it. The first thing to do in order to get the feel of it is to rock different chords in different rhythmic patterns. Using the C chord as an example, let the fourth finger

of your right hand strike and hold the note G above middle C,
while your thumb and forefinger strike the middle C and E above
middle C eight times.

You can sing, "Baby, baby, baby, baby" as you play this so that
you get the feel of the four beats that come on the first syllables.
After every two measures, you can repeat the G with your fourth
finger.

The next step is to use your left hand to accent the four beats
in each measure. You can do this by playing the first C below
middle C* on the first syllable of each "Baby." That would look
like this:

*Repeat last
two measures*

After doing this with the C chord, try "rocking" any other
chords—F or G chords, sevenths, minors, etc., until you feel
comfortable with the unsyncopated rock beat. At that point, try
rocking the syncopated version of "Give me a kiss, my baby" as
follows:

*See Appendix, page 135, for reading notes on bass clef.

STEP ONE

STEP TWO—BOTH HANDS

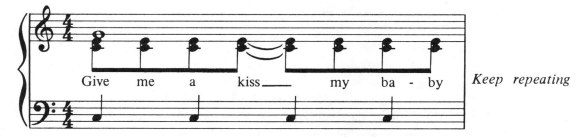

Note that in this example you play the third beat with your left hand even though your right will hold the tied notes. Accenting the third beat that way emphasizes the feeling of syncopation.

There are of course unlimited numbers of ways to syncopate chords within the rock style. You can use your left hand as an accomplice as well. For example, in the above version of "Give me a kiss," you could play the second C in the bass on the word "kiss" instead of on the second beat and tie it to the third. That would look like this:

*The left-hand bass notes in this and the following illustrations are the first C below middle C.

Here are some other patterns of syncopation you can try with any chords. Instead of spelling out actual notes, just the rhythmic patterns are represented here.

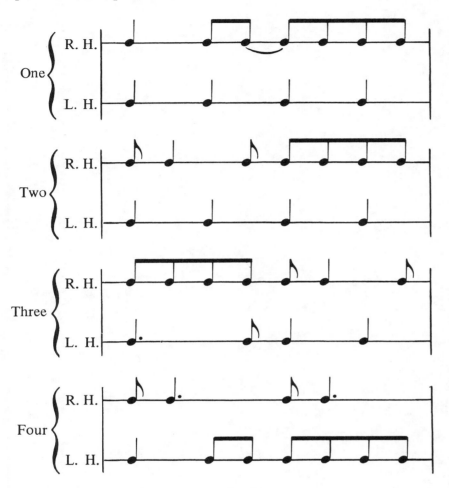

When you try the soft rock style as an accompaniment, you will find that you won't have to worry about syncopation. Chances are that the melodies themselves will provide the feeling of syncopation even though you are playing normally accented beats. That is because the lyrics have been fitted to syncopated music, and so when you follow their particular pattern of stresses, a feeling of syncopation will automatically result.

Finally, you can blend all the various styles together in your playing. As a matter of fact, there is a style called "classical-rock fusion," believe it or not! I believe that designation is self-explanatory. In any event, it shows how far you can go in combining different techniques.

LESSON 10

Playing by Ear and Improvising

HOW TO PLAY BY EAR

The ability to pick out the notes of melodies and harmonize them correctly without referring to any printed music as a guide is called playing by ear. Those who play by ear may not strike the right notes every time. But they are able to hear what is incorrect and then make proper adjustments with reasonable speed. Some people have ears so musically sensitive that after striking one particular note of a melody they will know exactly how many tones lower or higher the next note will be on the keyboard. Others may come reasonably close but will have to do some trial-and-error fumbling before hitting the right notes.

Of course experience is a key factor in finding the right keys. If you have trouble at first, don't be discouraged. You are bound to improve if you keep trying. I can make that statement with confidence because I know you are not tone deaf. If you were, you would certainly not be reading this book.

The step-by-step method that I will shortly detail for you will help you learn how to play by ear and will free you of the necessity to buy or borrow music in order to be able to play a particular piece. Further, even if you are content to play from the music, reading the following text will provide you with important principles of harmony that will greatly enhance your understanding of the music you play.

We will start with learning how to pick out melodies, and that means learning how to pick out the first notes on which they begin. Although melodies can be played in different keys (as you saw on page 53 with respect to "Twinkle, Twinkle, Little Star"), we will confine ourselves to the key of C. There are several reasons for using C as the key. First, it is good ear training to restrict yourself to a specified key rather than whatever you pick at random. Second, when you familiarize yourself with the chordal relationships that apply to C you will be better able to transpose later on.

Step one—*Pick out the first note of a song in the key of* C. As you saw on page 36, "Silent Night" begins on G, the fifth note of the scale, when played in the key of C. "Drink to Me" begins on E, the third note of the scale, as shown on page 42. "Twinkle, Twinkle, Little Star" begins on the first note, C, as shown in the first example on page 48. Thus, melodies can begin on different notes of the scale although they invariably end on the first, or tonic, note. They end that way because the tonic note is the note of ultimate resolution and gives a feeling of finality. Therefore, if you sing the *last* note of a particular song, you will know what key you are in. If the last note is a D, which is one tone higher than C, begin the song a tone lower and you will end up on C, the key you want to be in. You can tell what note you sang as the last by finding it on the piano. Just keep singing the note until you strike the right key on the piano. Strike the piano keys very softly while searching for the correct note so that you don't "lose" the pitch of the note you are singing.

As an exercise in picking out first notes, try "God Bless America." After that, try about ten different songs that you like and just get the right starting note in the key of C. I chose "God Bless America" as your first because it defines its tonality relatively quickly, so you may not have to wait until the end to hear the last note. You may hear it in your "mind's ear" well before that.

Also, it is a good melody to pick out in its entirety because it begins with one-step intervals and then has some leaps that will provide good practice in judging distances on the piano.

Step two—*Play entire melodies in the key of* C. I recommend that you try about twenty-five different tunes, playing each of them often enough so that you get to know them fairly well—not necessarily perfectly. (I know some very good pianists who have to do a quick review of the notes of a melody that they may have played for years but not recently.) Use your judgment as to how long you will continue with the second step before going on to the third. Some may want to stay with it a month or two, others only a day or two.

Step three—*Find the chords you need to harmonize the melody.* The best way to begin is to choose melodies that are built on the I, IV and V chords, that is, the tonic, subdominant and dominant chords, which are built on the first, fourth and fifth degrees of the scale. In the key of C those would be the C, F and G chords. Since it would be difficult for you to know what melodies are limited to those chords at this stage in your development, I have compiled a list from which you can choose the songs you would like to try.

At the start, I suggest that instead of playing the melody with your right hand, simply duplicate the chord, or some of its notes, and *sing* the melody. This will allow you to concentrate on choosing the correct chord, which is all you should concern yourself with now.

One other important point to bear in mind is this: The dominant chord will almost always sound better when played as a dominant seventh. In the key of C that chord would be a G7 and I suggest that you try it whenever you feel that the *dominant* harmony is the correct one.

Songs Using Only Tonic and Dominant Chords

"Alouette"	"The Muffin Man"
"The Farmer in the Dell"	"Lazy Mary"
"This Old Man"	
"Hush, Little Baby"	
"Oh, My Darling Clementine"	
"A Tisket, a Tasket"	

Songs Using Tonic, Dominant and Subdominant Chords
"God Bless America"
"Swing Low, Sweet Chariot"
"Yellow Submarine"
"Joy to the World"
"Home on the Range"
"Look to the Rainbow"
 Brahms's "Lullaby"
"Old Folks at Home"
"When the Saints Go Marching In"
"Ob-La-Di, Ob-La-Da"
"Happy Birthday to You"
"Amazing Grace"
"Oh, What a Beautiful Morning"

If you have successfully chosen the correct harmonies for these songs, you are well on the way to playing by ear. The next three steps you should take in learning to play by ear are listed below. Master each one before going on to the next.

Step four—*Play the melodies instead of just singing them.*

Step five—*Play the songs in keys other than C.* Review the tonic, subdominant and dominant chords in each key before you start in that particular key.

Step six—*Add whatever other chords you feel might heighten the harmonic interest of a song.* Sometimes a diminished chord will be useful as a transitional chord when you're going from the subdominant to the tonic. Sometimes a suspended seventh chord will sound better than its "unsuspended" form.

As pointed out in the "Harmonic" section of Lesson Nine, in popular songs you will very often find that progressions of chords follow the circle-of-fifths pattern. For example, in the key of C you will often find an A chord followed by a D chord which in turn is followed by a G chord. In fact, one of the most widely used progressions is the I, VI, II, V,* which in the key of C represents the C, Am7, Dm7 and G7 chords. I want to emphasize again that while the circle-of-fifths progression usually refers to

---

*In these progressions it matters little whether one chord is played higher or lower than another. What counts is the *sequence* of the *harmonies* involved.

dominant seventh chords, in a great deal of music there will be a mix of minor as well as dominant sevenths.

In looking through whatever music you have, note how often you will find the I, VI, II, V sequence; sometimes it will appear as II, V, I, VI or simply II, V, I. "Ain't Misbehavin'" begins with a I, VI, II, V sequence; so do "Blue Moon," "Heart and Soul," "The Way You Look Tonight," "Smoke Gets in Your Eyes," "Stormy Weather" and thousands of others. Learn the I, VI, II, V sequence in different keys and you will be able to play by ear with great facility.

HOW TO IMPROVISE

There are two ways that one can improvise. One is to simply play notes at random which, as a result of some experience and musical knowledge, produce pleasing musical effects. Sometimes new songs are created that way. A composer sits down at the piano and lets his fingers lead the way. Perhaps after playing some familiar chord progressions an "odd" chord is struck by accident; or a melody begins to evolve by letting the fingers of the right hand play random intervals interspersed with parts of scales or arpeggios. This kind of extemporaneous experimenting with the musical elements may be called *free* improvisation. No holds are barred, the only stricture being to make music, not noise.

The other form of improvisation is to invent variations that use a given piece of music as its frame of reference. These variations can be melodic as well as rhythmic and/or harmonic. Using "Twinkle, Twinkle, Little Star" in the key of C as the piece on which to "take off" or "jam," as jazz musicians would say, here is how each form of the three variations might be affected:

1. Melodic improvising Keeping the basic harmony intact (two measures of the tonic chord followed by one of the subdominant, then back to one of the tonic, etc.) the right hand might play a series of only the note C, perhaps using the C above middle C. Since C is a note that is common to the subdominant F chord, it will sound well when struck in the third measure. However, it would clash with the dominant G chord in the seventh measure, and so a G, B, D or F might be struck. This of course is about as elementary as one can get in giving an example of melodic variation. A slightly more advanced melodic variation could be achieved by playing different notes of the C chord in those measures where the C harmony prevails. The first word, "Twinkle," might be melodically varied by playing a G and an E for its two syllables; the second "twinkle" might use an E and a C, followed by an F and an A for the syllables of "little" in the third measure, etc.

A good beginning would be for you to play the chords of "Twinkle, Twinkle, Little Star" and try varying the melody. You don't necessarily have to stick to the exact notes of the chord, particularly on the weak beats of measures. The notes A, D and B♭, for example, sound good against C chords, as do D, G and E♭ against F chords. Experiment fearlessly and you will quickly learn what sounds good to you.

2. Rhythmic improvising A rhythmic variation of "Twinkle, Twinkle, Little Star" would be to play it in waltz time. In that case you might give two beats to the first syllable of "Twinkle" and one beat to the second. Your left hand would play a low C on the first syllable, followed by C chords higher up for the next two beats, the third coinciding with the second syllable of "Twinkle." The whole song can be played that way and I suggest that you try it.

"Twinkle" can also be played in a rock rhythm or block chord style. Although that melody is not one that you readily associate with those styles, it's fun to try them out for the sake of learning how to apply them.

3. Harmonic improvising A simple harmonic variation of "Twinkle" might be effected by applying the I, VI, II, V progression. Thus, instead of playing a C chord in the second measure, play an Am7. Then play a Dm7 in the third measure, followed by a G7sus and G7 for the two beats in the fourth measure.

A "far out" variation would be to play a D♭7 in the second measure followed by an E♭7 in the third, and back to D♭7 in the fourth. This could be continued by playing an A7aug in the fifth measure, a D7 in the sixth, a G7sus and G7 for the two notes of the seventh and back to the tonic in the eighth—or an A♭maj7 for a surprising ending to that phrase. As you will see when you try these variations, there is no limit to the different ways you can harmonize a melody.

One of the best ways to learn how to improvise is to use the twelve-measure blues progression. Each measure has four beats in a moderate tempo. In the key of C, the chords and beats would be indicated this way:

Chords: C   F   C   C7

Beats: / / / / | / / / / | / / / / | / / / / |

| F   / / / / | F   / / / / | C   / / / / | C   / / / / |

| G7 / / / / | F7 / / / / | C   / / / / | C (or G7) / / / / |

To begin with, just play the above chords with your left hand and tap the four beats with one foot. After you get the feel of this progression, which you can repeat as many times as you wish, you can start to add notes with your right hand. At first be sparing and add just a very few.

Also, you might try a technique which is called *crushing*. This is generally done by playing two adjacent notes simultaneously with the third and fourth fingers of your right hand. The notes in the C scale that are usually crushed are the E♭ with the E, which can be indicated as E♭/E; the G♭/G, A♭/A and B♭/B are often crushed as well. When crushing two notes, the technique is best accomplished by letting go of the lower of the two notes and holding the second. The higher of the two notes is the one that should be in harmony with the underlying chord. Thus, against an F chord you might crush A♭/A, not G♭/G.

In summary, when musicians improvise or jam they keep the framework of the chords intact, against which they play whatever notes they feel will create the dissonances or consonances that they want. Notes in the chord will create consonances; notes outside will generally, *but not always*, create dissonances. This gives you better than a fifty-fifty chance of hitting notes that will be musically compatible with the underlying chordal structure when you strike out at random.

When you start your improvisatory variations of your favorite songs, try to free yourself of any inhibitions with respect to hitting wrong notes. If you hit a "sour" note, chances are that if you keep repeating it, it will begin to sweeten. That happens to be a fortuitous property that music seems to have—and thank God!

It is extremely helpful to have another instrument playing along with you when you improvise. There are several reasons for this: the rhythm of the piece will be more easily kept; one can play the harmony while the other fools with the melody, and vice versa; the feeling of syncopation is easier to effect because when each instrumentalist produces accents independently, they won't be simultaneous at all times. At any rate, you learn from each other when improvising together and it can be enormous fun.

A FINAL NOTE

When I first planned the contents of this book I thought I might end each lesson with a brief summary. I thought perhaps that I might even have a short quiz which could be called "Key Questions" to which of course I would supply "Noteworthy Answers." What a clever idea it seemed at the time!

However, before I got to the second or third lesson I realized that I could not summarize, or make more succinct, that which already aimed to be the concisest of explanations of popular piano playing. I had set out to present a "no frills" course, meaning above all, no drills!

However, I would like to offer one suggestion that I think can be of enormous help: Please reread the lessons at least once, especially if you have had little or no background in music theory. The contents of this book may be compared to a jigsaw puzzle— you work with each piece, but you don't know what the finished puzzle will depict. So while you are gathering the individual pieces of information, you might not know exactly where they fit or what their future meaning may be. However, once you know the outcome—see the picture as a whole—each of the individual parts will be understood in its proper context and will interlock perfectly with all the other facts you have learned. In the words of my dear friend Sammy Cahn, there are things in life that become better "The Second Time Around."

APPENDIX

CHECKLIST OF CHORD SYMBOLS

C   C Major Chord (or Triad)

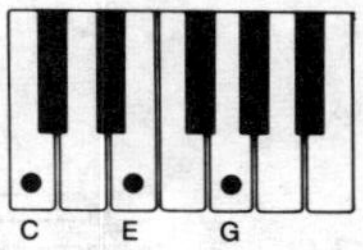

Cm    C Minor Chord (or Triad)

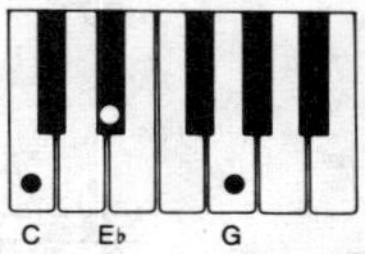

Cdim    C Diminished Chord (or Triad)

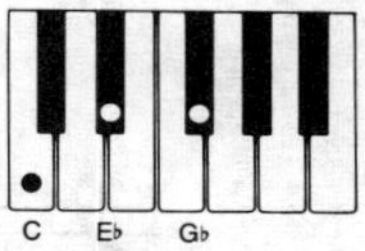

Caug or C+    C Augmented Chord (or Triad)

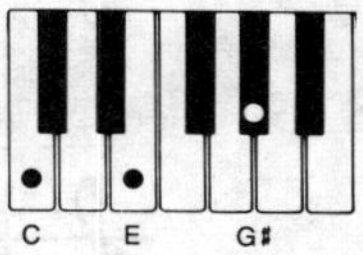

Csus or Csus4    C Suspended Fourth Chord (or Triad)

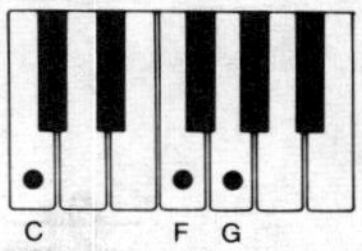

C6    C Major Sixth Chord

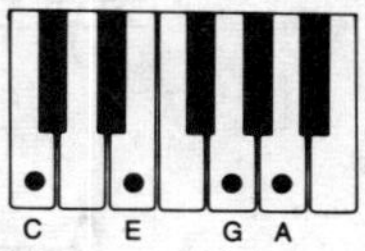

Cm6    C Minor Sixth Chord

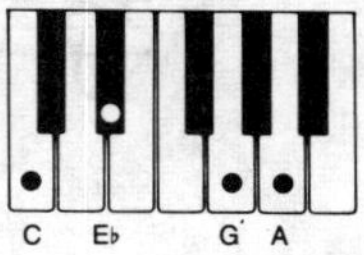

Cmaj7    C Major Seventh Chord

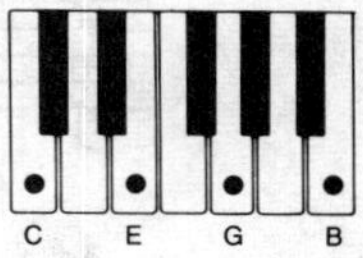

Cm7    C Minor Seventh Chord

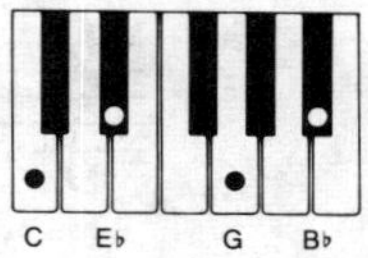

C7    C Dominant Seventh Chord

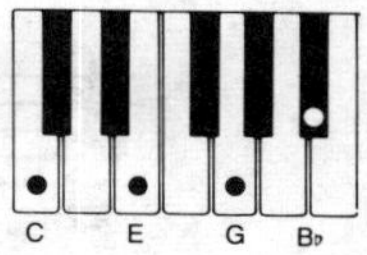

131

Cdim7 — C Diminished Seventh Chord

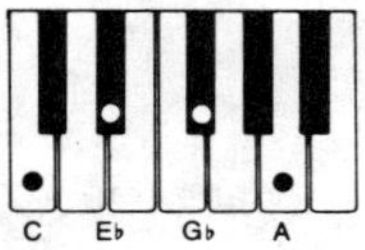

C Eb Gb A

Caug7 or C7+  — C Augmented Seventh Chord

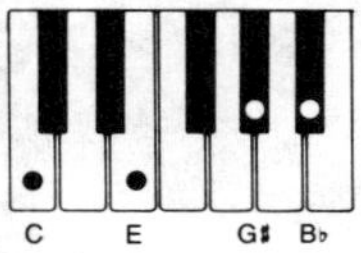

C E G# Bb

C7sus or C7sus4  — C Suspended Seventh Chord

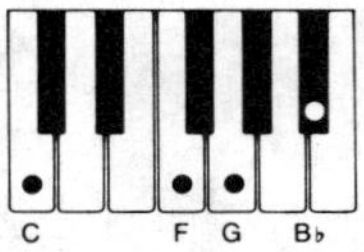

C F G Bb

C7b5 — C Seventh Flat Five Chord

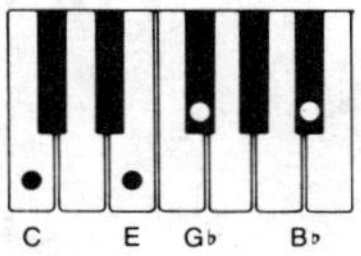

C E Gb Bb

C7b9 — C Seventh Plus Flat Nine Chord

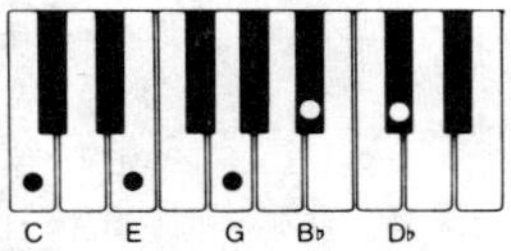

C E G Bb Db

C9  — C Ninth Chord

C E G Bb D

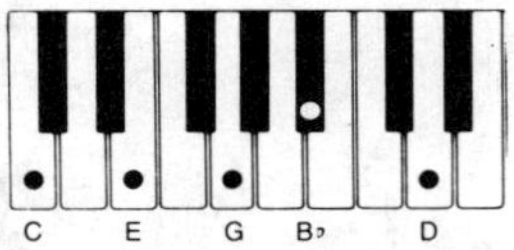

Cm9  — C Minor Ninth Chord

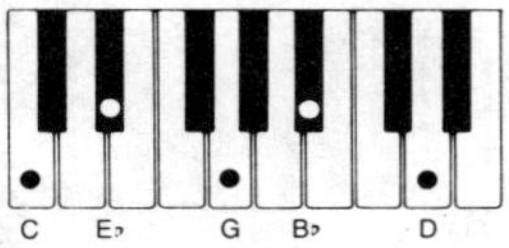

C Eb G Bb D

C11  — C Eleventh Chord

C E G Bb D F

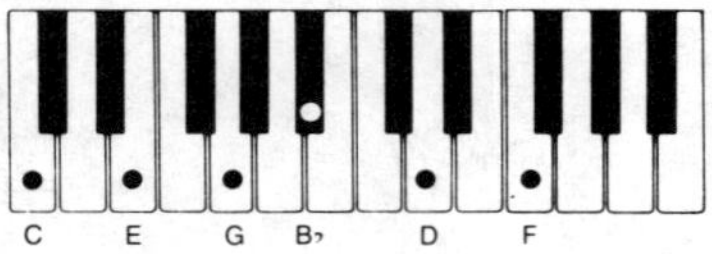

C13 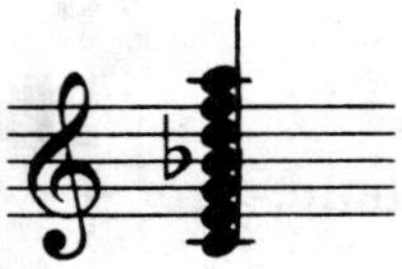 — C Thirteenth Chord

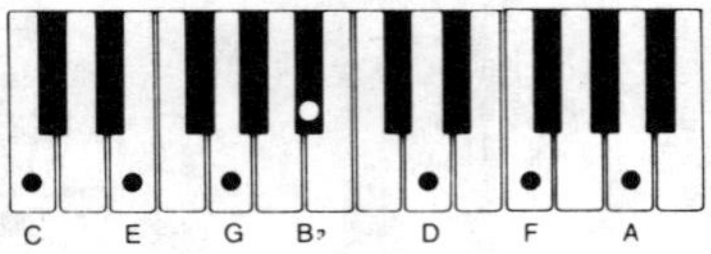

C E G Bb D F A

C/E  — C Chord with E in Bass

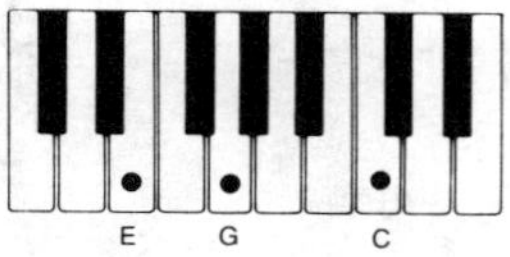

E G C

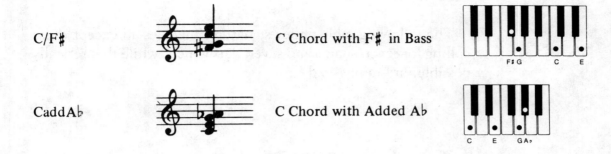

C/F♯ — C Chord with F♯ in Bass

CaddA♭ — C Chord with Added A♭

MINOR MATTERS

In explaining how to form minor chords it was possible to do so without reference to the notes of the minor scale. Once you know how to change a major chord into the minor by lowering the third, you have obviated the necessity of spelling out the notes of the minor scale. However, as far as the *meaning* of the minor mode is concerned, here are some "minor matters" which I hope will have a major impact on your understanding of tonality.

First, you may notice that if you play a C major chord, for example, and then change it to C minor the sound becomes less cheerful. As a matter of fact the usual adjectives for minor harmonies are melancholy, wistful, sad—even gloomy—whereas major harmonies are spoken of as being bright, cheerful and, on the whole, upbeat. The most dramatic way I know of to demonstrate the difference between major and minor tonalities is to take a song one is accustomed to hearing in the major and change it to minor—a sound is worth a thousand words.

Below are the first eight measures of "Twinkle, Twinkle, Little Star" changed from the key of C major to C minor. Play it and see what a difference a mode makes.

KEY SIGNATURES

The following table of key signatures includes all except those calling for seven sharps and seven flats which, while theoretically possible, are rarely used.

The signatures for the keys of Gb or F#, in the major mode, result in the same keys being struck on the piano. Therefore a piece of music written in either key will sound exactly the same. (The same is true of course for the keys of Eb or D# in the minor mode.) A change from Gb to F# is called an *enharmonic* change, meaning that the notes are the same although spelled differently. For example, a composer writing for the guitar would use an F# rather than a Gb since guitarists find it easier to think in terms of sharps. On the other hand, in writing for the clarinet a composer would more than likely use the Gb.

You might wonder how to tell if a piece is in the major or minor key, since the signatures are the same. The difference in sound between the two is of course unmistakable, as you can tell if you played the minor-key version of "Twinkle, Twinkle." When the chords of your songs are designated in symbols, you can usually tell at a glance. For example, if you find three flats in the signature and see symbols for C minor, F minor and G seventh chords (as opposed to Eb major and Bb sevenths) you can bet that the song is in C minor and not Eb major. In some cases songs may be in the minor mode half the time and major the other half; in other words, in *both* keys. Cole Porter used to like to compose that way. For example, "I Love Paris" begins in C minor and ends in C major. All that really matters is that you know how to play the chords, whether they be major or minor.

MUSIC NOTATION

Some aspects of music notation have been explained in the first few chapters. As far as the goals of this book are concerned, all the essential details of music notation have been covered. However, for the sake of those who might be interested in learning how to read the bass clef staff, as well as rests and dotted notes, etc., the following supplementary information is presented.

The Staff and The Clefs Music for the piano is written on two staves (the plural of "staff"). Treble clef is for the right hand and bass clef for the left. This combination of staves is called the *great staff*.

THE GREAT STAFF

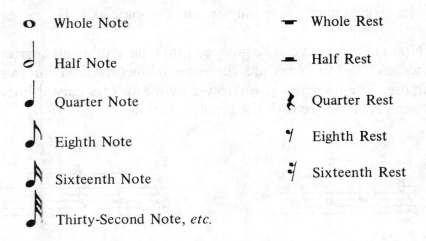

For notation of sharps and flats see lesson four.

Notes and Rests The position of a note on the staff indicates its *pitch*. The design of a note (whether hollow, filled in, stemmed, etc.) indicates its time value or *duration*. Rests are characters whose time values correspond to the various notes, and indicate periods of silence.

𝅝 Whole Note	▬ Whole Rest
𝅗𝅥 Half Note	▬ Half Rest
𝅘𝅥 Quarter Note	𝄽 Quarter Rest
𝅘𝅥𝅮 Eighth Note	𝄾 Eighth Rest
𝅘𝅥𝅯 Sixteenth Note	𝄿 Sixteenth Rest
𝅘𝅥𝅰 Thirty-Second Note, *etc.*	

Notes that have *tails* (eighths, sixteenths, etc.) may be joined together by *beams:* ♪ ♪ *or* ♫   ♪ ♪ *or* ♫

If a quarter note (♩) is entitled to *one* beat, as is usually the case, a whole note (o) would be entitled to *four* beats, a half note (♩) to *two*. Eighth notes (♪ ♪ *or* ♫) would equal a *half* beat (meaning two eighth notes to *one* beat) as illustrated along with the other note values:

Rests have the same duration (number of beats) as the notes that correspond to their values.

Dots are used to extend the duration of notes by one-half their original value. Thus a dotted half note (♩.) would be equal to three quarter notes (♩ ♩ ♩); a dotted quarter note would equal three eighths (♫ ♪). Rests are similarly increased in value by the use of dots. Thus ▬. equals ▬♪♪. Dots are shortcuts for the use of ties. For example, ♩. is simpler, but the same as ♩ ♩.

Notes of any kind can be grouped into *triplets* although quarter notes and eighth notes are the most frequently used for this purpose. The designation is effected by means of a curved line, or bracket, together with the number 3, thus:

A *triplet* is a group of three notes to be performed within the same time span that two notes of the same denomination would normally take. Thus in the first example the three eighth notes would be played in the time span normally alloted to two eighth notes. If two eighth notes would be entitled to one beat (as is usual in most popular music) then a triplet comprised of three eighth notes would be entitled to one beat.

In the second example the three quarter notes have the duration of two quarters, the same as a half note.

Time Signatures Music is divided into sections called measures in order to show its rhythm or *beat*. Fractions are used at the beginning to indicate the unit value of each measure, the most common fractions being ²⁄₄, ³⁄₄ and ⁴⁄₄. For example, music in three-quarter time (denoted by ³⁄₄) means that each measure has a total time value equal to three quarter notes. "The Blue Danube Waltz" might be written as follows:

In the example above, each beat is represented by the value of a quarter note. This is customary in modern times, although it is not always done. For example, it would be mathematically correct to write "The Blue Danube" in ³⁄₈ time, in which case each beat would have the value of an eighth note:

The important thing is to understand the value of the notes in terms of their relation to each other. In other words, if you give one beat to a quarter note, you must know that a half note will be entitled to two beats and a whole note to four. Or, if you give one beat to an eighth note, you must give two beats to each quarter note, etc. Once you grasp that principle you will be able to read any piece of music in correct time.

Other Signs and Symbols The numerous signs and symbols that are used in music notation are enough to fill a book this size or larger. In the kind of popular music that falls within the province of this book, you are not likely to run across any that you won't be able to figure out by using plain, ordinary common sense. However, there are a few that are worth special mention since they are used so frequently.

Quite often in songs the music remains the same but the lyrics change. For example, in "Drink to Me Only With Thine Eyes" (page 42) the melody repeats itself after the first eight measures although the words are different. The repetition of the music could have been indicated by the commonly used symbol of two dots before a double bar, :‖ . This is a repeat sign, and it instructs you to go back to the beginning. Notice its use in the eighth measure of the following example:

1. Drink to me on - ly with ___ thine eyes ___ and I ___ will
2. Or leave a kiss with - in ___ the cup ___ and I'll ___ not

pledge with mine. ___
ask for

wine. ___ The thirst ___ that *etc.*

Notice also that over the seventh and eighth measures you see this sign: ⌐1.⌐ followed by ⌐2.⌐ over the next two measures. This means you should play the measures marked ⌐1.⌐ the first time through, but after the repeat, skip them and continue with the *second ending*, marked ⌐2.⌐

If you come across an inverted repeat sign, ‖:, at some point after the beginning of the music, then that is where you start the repeat instead of going back to the very beginning. For example, in "Silent Night" (page 36) the music of the thirteenth, fourteenth, fifteenth and sixteenth measures is the same as the ninth, tenth, eleventh and twelfth. Although shortcuts aren't used for such brief repetitions, for illustrative purposes this is how it would appear:

Obviously, when you repeat the music of the ninth through the twelfth measures, you sing the words following number 2, having sung number 1 the first time.

In that same example you will observe a series of dots (a dotted curve) above the notes of the ninth measure, whereas on page 36 you will find a slur over those notes. The reason is this: On page 36 the ninth measure involves only the word "Virgin" of which the first syllable requires two notes. The slur indicates that the two notes embraced by it stand for just one syllable. In the above example, however, those notes involve the word "infant" as well as "Virgin," and in the case of "Infant" *each* syllable gets a note. The dotted curve indicates that a slur is not required in both instances.

The meaning of two other repeat signs is described best in Howard Shanet's excellent book entitled *Learn to Read Music*, and the following is a verbatim quotation:

> Sometimes, especially in long pieces, the composer will indicate a repeat by writing *D.C.*, which is an abbreviation for the Italian words *da capo*, meaning "from the head" or "from the top." If he wants you to go back to some special point, but not all the way to the beginning, he may mark

that special point with a sign, either ⊕ or 𝄋 , and write *D.S.* which is an abbreviation for the Italian words *dal segno*, meaning "from the sign."

If the phrase *al fine* ("to the end") is added (*D.C. al fine*, or *D.S. al fine*), it means that you are to go back to the beginning or to the sign, as the case may be, but repeat only until you reach the word *Fine* ("end") written in the music. Here are two examples each of which includes an ordinary repeat sign as well as a *D.C.* or *D.S.*:

The Marine's Hymn

Old Folks At Home

Notice that in "The Marine's Hymn" the repeat instructions occur after only part of the measure has gone by (i.e., there are only three beats, instead of the four which we expect in ⁴/₄ meter, in the last printed measure where the D.C. appears). A *Da Capo*, a *Dal Segno*, or an ordinary repeat sign need not come at the end of a measure; it may be used anywhere within the measure. This is especially frequent in pieces which begin with an upbeat, as "The Marine's Hymn" does.

The last word to be explained, quite aptly coming at the end of this appendix, is *coda*. This designates a "last word" or concluding section of a piece of music that is often extraneous to its basic structure. In popular songs it is often an eight-measure phrase that you are asked to "repeat and fade," the way many recordings of songs do at the end.

You are usually directed to the coda at a given point in the song (which you have arrived at for the second or third time) by the sign ⊕ over the end of the measure from which you are to proceed to the coda, also marked by the same sign. For example, after playing the first chorus of a song, you are directed to *D.S. al Coda* ⊕. That means you should go back to wherever the sign 𝄋 appears and repeat the music until you reach the direction *To Coda* ⊕ at which point you will skip to the coda, usually labeled in this manner: Coda ⊕.